Ground Beef "Round-Up"

Edited by Annette Gohlke, Food Editor

Illustrations by Peggy Bjorkman

Layout Artist: Janet Kumbier

Production: Sally Radtke, Sue DesRochers

Cover Photography by Mike Hubregtse

Library of Congress Catalog Card Number: 79-56741
ISBN 0-89821-032-1

733 North Van Buren
Milwaukee, Wisconsin 53202

From Our Kitchen...

Dear Friends:

This mouth-watering "Ground Beef Round-Up" cookbook is the fourteenth in our series of specialized cookbooks that feature the recipes of the best cooks in the world—farm wives. All 180 recipes have been farm kitchen tested. The cookbook also includes the winners in our Farm Wife News magazine's "Rural Recipe Round-Up" ground beef contest.

The response to our initial call for ground beef recipes was tremendous—proving once again that good ol' ground beef—or to put it more plainly, hamburger—is America's favorite meat. The U.S.A. has certainly put hamburger on the meat map—more ground beef is eaten today than any other type of meat.

From the kids on up to grandma and grandpa, ground beef is enjoyed for one reason—it's always so-o-o-o-o good! Plus, it's easy to eat, versatile in many different dishes and so easy to prepare.

Within this cookbook, you'll find a dazzling array of 180 ground beef recipes—ranging from appetizers to casseroles, chili, soups, stews, hamburgers, steaks, sandwiches, meatballs, meat loaf, ethnic recipes and a whole potpourri of unusual recipes featuring ground beef.

We're sure this cookbook will soon be one of the most used cookbooks in your kitchen! And once again, we owe our sincere thanks to all of our faithful Farm Wife News readers who contributed their favorites to our recipe contests. These women always readily share their family-favorite recipes and are constantly on the lookout for new, delicious dishes to serve to their families.

As you page through the many ground beef recipes in this book, we know you'll feel you are right in "hamburger heaven". So have a good time broiling, frying, grilling and baking ground beef via the recipes you'll enjoy in this book. We know that you'll all agree that "ground beef is great."

Annette Gohlke

FWN Food Editor

Contents

Appetizers

HAMBURGER DIP

1/2 pound ground beef
1/2 cup chopped onion
1/2 cup taco sauce
1 teaspoon chili powder
1 can kidney beans, drained, mashed
1/4 cup shredded cheddar cheese
1/4 cup chopped onion
1/4 cup sliced green olives

Brown beef and onion. Add taco sauce, chili powder and mashed beans; mix well. Spoon into baking dish, top with combined cheese, onion and olives. Warm in 350° oven. Serve with taco chips.

Mrs. Jerry Breidenback, Iliff, Colorado

TAMALE BITES

2 cups crumbled corn bread
10-ounce can mild enchilada sauce, divided
1/2 teaspoon salt
1-1/2 pounds ground beef
8 ounces tomato sauce
1/2 cup shredded cheese (half Monterey Jack and half cheddar)

Combine corn bread crumbs, 1/2 cup enchilada sauce, salt and beef. Mix well and shape into 1-in. balls. Place in shallow baking dish; bake uncovered at 350° 18 to 20 minutes. Place in chafing dish to keep warm. Meanwhile, heat the tomato sauce and remaining enchilada sauce; pour over meatballs and top with shredded cheese. Serve as appetizers. Yield: About 90 meatballs.

Charlotte Loveless, Sullivan, Indiana

BEEF ITALIA FONDUE

1 pound ground beef
15 ounces spaghetti sauce
12 ounces cheddar cheese, cubed
4 ounces mozarella cheese, cubed
1 tablespoon cornstarch
1/2 cup cooking wine
Dash garlic salt
Small can chopped mushrooms, drained
French bread

Brown beef in skillet. Add remaining ingredients to beef. Simmer gently until cheeses are melted. Pour into fondue pot; keep warm. Dip chunks of French bread into fondue.

Linda L. Reinert, Reading, Pennsylvania

CHEEZY BEEF ON RYE

1-1/2 pounds ground beef
1 pound pork sausage
1 teaspoon garlic salt
1 teaspoon oregano
1 pound Velvetta cheese, diced
1 loaf thin sliced party rye bread

Saute ground beef and pork sausage until brown. Drain fat. Add seasoning and cheese; stir until cheese is melted. Spread on slices of rye bread; bak under broiler for 3 minutes. *Mrs. Bernice Burbach, Eau Claire, Michiga*

SPICY BEEF DIP

1 pound ground beef
1/2 cup chopped onion
1 clove garlic OR garlic powder
8 ounces tomato sauce
1/4 cup catsup
1 teaspoon sugar
3/4 teaspoon oregano
8 ounces cream cheese, softened
1/3 cup Parmesan cheese

Saute beef and onion until lightly browned. Stir in garlic, tomato sauce, cat sup, sugar and oregano. Cover and simmer 10 minutes. Add cheeses; stirrin until cheese melts. Keep warm in chafing dish. Serve with crackers or di chips. *Mrs. Wayne Fitscher, Lake City, Minnesot*

PIZZA TREATS

1-1/2 pounds ground beef
1 envelope onion soup mix
1 egg
1 loaf snack size rye bread
6-ounce jar Ragu sauce (spaghetti sauce)
8 ounces mozarella cheese

Mix ground beef, onion soup mix and egg, blending well. Spread mixture o slices of rye bread. Spread 1 teaspoon sauce over beef; place small piece o cheese over sauce and place bread on cookie sheet. Bake at 350° until mea is done to your liking and cheese is melted.

Mrs. Albert Rehak, Denmark, Wisconsi

PERKED UP CHEESE: *When a recipe calls for sharp flavored cheese an you only have a mild flavored cheese on hand, here's a clever use of season ings. Add a little dry mustard, dash of pepper and Worchestershire sauce, blend into cheese.* *Mrs. Alice Waters, Arcadia, Wisconsi*

Casseroles

BEEF CASSEROLE

1 pound ground beef
1 onion, chopped
1/2 teaspoon garlic salt
Salt and pepper
15-ounce can spaghetti
1 pound red kidney beans, drained
1 can tomato soup
1 can onion rings (French fried)

Brown beef, and onion; season with garlic salt, salt and pepper to taste. Add spaghetti, beans and soup; mix well. Pour into baking dish and top with onion rings. Bake at 350° about 35 minutes.

Mrs. Dori Huenefeld, Aurora, Nebraska

BEEF AND CORN AU GRATIN

2 pounds ground beef
1 medium size onion, chopped
1/4 teaspoon salt
1/4 teaspoon pepper
1 teaspoon sage
1 teaspoon seasoned salt
1/8 teaspoon nutmeg
7-ounce can whole kernel corn, drained
8-ounce can tomato sauce
1 medium tomato, chopped
2 green peppers, slivered
1-1/2 cup bread crumbs OR crushed seasoned croutons
1 cup shredded cheddar cheese
1 teaspoon onion salt
2 teaspoons parsley flakes

Fry beef and onion until browned. Add seasonings, corn, tomato sauce, tomato and peppers. Cover and simmer 15 minutes. Pour mixture into 2-1/2 quart casserole. Combine crumbs, cheese, onion salt and parsley. Sprinkle over top. Bake at 350° about 20 minutes until casserole ingredients are bubbly hot and crumbs are browned. *Mrs. Fred Bolt, Hesperia, Michigan*

BEEF AND POTATO CASSEROLE

2 slices diced bacon
4 medium-sized potatoes
1 pound ground beef
1 medium-sized onion, chopped
10-3/4-ounce can spaghetti sauce

Saute bacon until crisp. Add peeled, thinly sliced raw potatoes. Cover and cook slowly 10 minutes, stirring occasionally. Sprinkle with salt and pepper. Place in 1-1/2-quart baking dish. In same skillet, brown beef and onion. Salt and pepper to taste. Spread over potatoes. Cover with spaghetti sauce. Bake at 350° about 45 minutes. *Mrs. Vernon Coe, Sr., Windham, New York*

GROUND BEEF ZUCCHINI CASSEROLE

2 pounds zucchini
1-1/4 pounds ground beef
1 onion, chopped
1 green pepper, slivered
1 teaspoon salt
Dash pepper
1/2 pound Velvetta cheese, diced
1 can mushroom soup
1/2 cup buttered crumbs

Wash zucchini, cut off stem end. Do not peel, unless squash is large and skin is tough. Cut in 1/2-in. slices; cook 4 minutes, drain. Brown beef, onion and green pepper. Season with salt and pepper. Layer meat, squash and cheese in 2-quart greased casserole or baking dish. Spread undiluted soup over top. Bake at 350° 30 minutes. Sprinkle buttered crumbs over top of casserole, bake 15 minutes more. *Mrs. Sidney Lorence, Racine, Wisconsin*

COMPANY PERFECT CASSEROLE

2 pounds ground beef
1/2 cup dairy sour cream
3 tablespoons dry onion soup mix
1 egg, beaten
1-1/2 cups soft bread crumbs
1/3 cup flour
1 teaspoon paprika
8-ounce can whole or sliced mushrooms
1 can cream of chicken soup
1 can cream of mushroom soup
2 cups water

Butter Crumb Dumplings:
2 cups flour
4 teaspoons baking powder
1 tablespoon poppy seeds
1 teaspoon celery salt
1 teaspoon poultry seasoning
2 teaspoons dry onion flakes
1/4 cup oil
3/4 cup plus 2 tablespoons milk
1/4 cup melted butter
2 cups soft bread crumbs

Combine beef, sour cream, onion soup mix, egg and 1-1/2 cups bread crumbs. Shape into 16 meat balls. Roll in flour-paprika mixture and brown slowly in hot, greased skillet. Combine mushrooms, (use liquid as part of water), soups and water, pour over meatballs; simmer 20 minutes. Place meatballs and gravy in 3-quart casserole. **Dumplings:** Combine flour, baking powder, poppy seeds and seasonings. Blend in oil and milk, stirring only until dry mixture is moist. Stir melted butter into bread crumbs. Drop tablespoonfuls of dough into crumbs, tossing to coat. Place on top of hot casserole mixture. Bake, uncovered, at 400° 20 to 25 minutes, or until dumplings are golden. Serves 8 to 10. *Bonnie Reinhardt, Bunker Hill, Kansas*

STUFFED GREEN PEPPERS

6 green peppers
1 cup Wheaties cereal flakes
1 cup tomato juice
1 egg
1 small onion, chopped
1 pound ground beef
Salt and pepper to taste
Catsup

Cut top from green peppers, clean out seeds. Parboil peppers in salted water 5 minutes; drain well. Soften cereal in tomato juice, beat in egg. Add onion and ground beef; mix well. Season to taste. Fill peppers with meat mixture. Place in greased casserole dish, sized to hold peppers. Pour about 1/2-in. water in bottom of dish. Top each pepper with catsup. Bake at 350° 1 hour.

Mrs. Wavalea Oliver, St. Joseph, Missouri

GROUND BEEF SAUERKRAUT CASSEROLE

1 pound ground beef
1 small onion, chopped
1 teaspoon salt
1/4 teaspoon pepper
16-ounce can sauerkraut, drained
2 cups noodles, cooked
1 can cream of celery soup
1 can cream of mushroom soup
4-ounce can mushrooms, drained
1 cup grated cheese

Brown beef and onion; season with salt and pepper; drain fat. Layer half of beef in 13- x 9-in. baking dish. Cover with sauerkraut then remaining beef. Spread cooked noodles over meat. Combine soups and mushrooms; spread over noodles. Bake at 350° 30 minutes. Sprinkle cheese over top of casserole; bake 30 minutes more. *Jolene Caldwell, Council Bluffs, Iowa*

CHEESEY BEEF HOT DISH

1 pound frozen French fries
1 pound ground beef
1 onion, chopped
1/2 cup water
2 teaspoons salt
1/2 teaspoon pepper
8-1/2-ounce can peas, drained
10-1/2-ounce cream of mushroom soup
3/4 cup small curd cottage cheese
3/4 cup cubed cheddar cheese
1/2 teaspoon paprika

Place French fries in greased 3-quart casserole. Brown beef, onion, water, salt and pepper. Add peas, soup and cottage cheese. Mix gently; pour over potatoes. Bake at 350° 45 minutes. Sprinkle top with cheddar cheese, bake 5 minutes more to melt cheese. Dust top with paprika.

Mrs. Nova Vellema, Waupun, Wisconsin

LOW CALORIE CASSEROLE

1 small cabbage, chopped or sliced
1 cup sliced carrots, optional
1 pound ground beef
1 onion, chopped
Salt and pepper to taste
1/3 cup uncooked rice
10-1/2-ounce can cream of tomato soup
1 cup water

Brown beef and onion; drain fat. Salt and pepper. Stir in rice. In greased baking dish, layer chopped or sliced cabbage. Sprinkle with salt. Layer carrots over cabbage; salt. Spread beef over vegetables. Mix soup and water; pour over meat. Cover and bake at 350° 1 hour.

Wanda Mast, Millersburg, Ohio

FIVE LAYER DISH

1 pound ground beef
1 small onion, chopped
2 cups sliced raw potatoes
2 cups sliced raw carrots
2 cups cut green beans
Several slices American cheese, diced
10-1/2-ounce can tomato soup
Crushed potato chips

Brown beef and onion, season with salt and pepper to taste. In 2-1/2-quart casserole dish layer potatoes, carrots, beans and meat. Lightly salt each layer of vegetables. Sprinkle cheese over top. Spread soup over top, then crushed chips. Bake at 350° 50 to 60 minutes until vegetables are tender.

Mrs. Marilyn K. Hayek, Friend, Nebraska

BEEF 'N RICE CASSEROLE

1-1/2 pounds ground beef
1/2 cup finely chopped onion
1 small bay leaf
1 teaspoon salt
Dash pepper
1-pound can stewed tomatoes
1 can cream of mushroom soup
1 cup raw Minute Rice
1/8 teaspoon garlic powder
1/8 teaspoon thyme
1/8 teaspoon oregano
4 sliced, stuffed olives
3 slices American cheese

Brown beef and onion; drain fat. Stir in remaining ingredients except olives and cheese. Bring mixture to boil, reduce heat; cover and simmer 10 minutes, stirring occasionally. Place mixture in serving dish, decorate with olives and triangles of cheese.

Mrs. Sharon Hedgpeth, South Holland, Illinois

CABBAGE CASSEROLE

4 cups shredded cabbage
1-1/2 pounds ground beef
3 tablespoons chopped onion
1/4 teaspoon pepper
1/8 teaspoon garlic salt
1/2 cup uncooked rice
1-1/2 teaspoons salt
1/2 teaspoon paprika
6-ounce can tomato paste
2 cups water
1 cup dairy sour cream
Topping of canned biscuits OR bread crumbs

Spread cabbage in 13- x 9-in. greased baking dish. Mix ground beef with onion, pepper, garlic salt, rice, salt and paprika; spread over cabbage. Mix tomato paste with water; pour over meat mixture. Cover with foil; bake at 300° 1-1/2 hours. Remove from oven; spread top with sour cream. Top with biscuits sprinkled with parsley. Bake at 400° 8 to 10 minutes to brown biscuits.

Mrs. Glen Kaufmann, Orrville, Ohio

FARMER'S DELIGHT

1 pound ground beef
1 garlic clove, minced
1 large onion, chopped
1 green pepper, chopped
Salt and pepper to taste
10-1/2-ounce can cream of tomato soup
8-ounce cream style corn
6 to 8 ounces canned chopped mushrooms
1 teaspoon Worcestershire sauce
10-ounce package spaghetti
1 cup shredded cheddar cheese

Brown beef, garlic, onion, green pepper. Salt and pepper to taste. Meanwhile, cook spaghetti, drain well. Combine meat, spaghetti and remaining ingredients, except cheese. Reserve 1/3 cup cheese, add rest to casserole. Pour mixture into 2-1/2-quart casserole, sprinkle top with reserved cheese. Bake at 350° 45 minutes or until casserole is bubbly hot.

Mrs. Gerd R. Hein, Gifford, Illinois

WHITE CAKE WITH CHOCOLATE FROSTING

1-1/2 pounds ground beef
1 medium onion, diced
Salt and pepper
Dash chili powder
1 teaspoon oregano
8 ounces tomato sauce
2 cups macaroni
6 ounces cheddar cheese, grated
3 eggs
3/4 cup milk

Brown beef and onion. Season to taste. Add tomato sauce; simmer gently 30 minutes. Cook macaroni according to directions. Place meat mixture in bottom of 2-quart casserole. Mix cheese with cooked macaroni; spread over meat mixture. Beat eggs with milk; pour over macaroni. Bake at 350° 1 hour—do not cover! To serve, invert on warm serving plate.

Mrs. Carol Martinson, Brooklyn, Wisconsin

SPAGHETTI CUPS FOR TWO

3-pound spaghetti squash
1 pound ground beef
1 small onion, chopped
1 teaspoon Italian seasoning
Garlic salt
8 ounces tomato sauce
4 ounces mozzarella cheese, shredded

Cut the stem off spaghetti squash. Boil whole for 5 minutes in covered Dutch oven. Slice in half, lengthwise and scoop out seeds. Place the two halves in 12- x 8-in. baking dish. Fill dish with 1/2-in. of water. Brown beef and onion in skillet. Stir in seasoning and garlic salt to taste. Fill squash halves with meat. Carefully pour tomato sauce over meat. Sprinkle top with shredded cheese. Bake at 350° 30 minutes. Check after baking 15 minutes. If dry, pour small amount of water or tomato sauce over squash.

Melissa Hirst, Woodstock, Illinois

STUFFED EGGPLANT

2 1-pound eggplants
1/2 pound ground beef
1 large onion, chopped fine
1 medium tomato, chopped
3 cloves garlic, crushed (or to taste)
3 tablespoons oil
Minced parsley
1 teaspoon salt
1/2 teaspoon pepper
1/2 teaspoon oregano
1 cup water
4 ounces cheddar cheese

Cut eggplants in half lengthwise. Scoop out flesh leaving about 1/4-in. shell with skin. Cut pulp in 1/2-in. cubes. In 12-in. skillet cook and stir eggplant pulp, beef, onion, tomato and garlic in hot oil until beef is browned and onion is tender. Stir in 1/4 cup parsley and seasonings. Fill eggplant shells with meat mixture. Place eggplant in 13- x 9-in. baking dish. Pour water in bottom of dish. Cover with foil and bake at 350° 30 minutes. Top eggplant with cheese strips; bake 5 minutes more. Garnish eggplant with additional parsley.

Mrs. H.S. Cornell, Ballston Spa, New York

IBURGER CORN CASSEROLE

- 1-1/2 pounds ground beef
- 1 cup chopped onion
- 12-ounce can whole kernel corn
- 10-1/2-ounce can cream of chicken soup
- 10-1/2-ounce can cream of mushroom soup
- 1 cup sour cream
- 1/4 cup chopped pimiento
- 1 teaspoon salt
- 1/4 teaspoon pepper
- 3 cups cooked noodles
- 3 tablespoons butter
- 1 cup soft bread crumbs

Lightly brown beef and onions; drain fat. Add remaining ingredients except butter and bread crumbs. Pour into 2-1/2-quart casserole. Melt butter, pour over crumbs; mix to blend. Sprinkle over meat mixture. Bake at 350° 30 minutes or until mixture is bubbly hot and crumbs are browned.

Mrs. E. K. Kirby, Capron, Virginia

BARB CUPS

- 2 rolls canned biscuits
- 1 pound ground beef
- 1/3 cup diced onion
- Salt to taste
- 1/2 cup barbecue sauce
- Grated cheese

Brown beef and onion; drain fat. Add salt and barbecue sauce; simmer gently about 15 minutes. Grease 20 muffin cups. Place 1 biscuit in each cup, shaping with fingers to fit muffin cup. Spoon meat mixture into biscuit cups filling about 3/4 full. Sprinkle top with cheese. Bake at 375° 15 minutes.

Cleta M. Deppe, Bellevue, Iowa

BEEF DRESSING CASSEROLE

- 12 slices bread, cubed
- 1/2 cup chopped onion
- 1 cup chopped celery
- Salt and pepper to taste
- Sage or poultry seasoning to taste
- 1 can cream of celery soup
- 1 cup milk
- 2 pounds ground beef
- 1 tablespoon prepared mustard
- 1 tablespoon Worcestershire sauce
- 1 can cream of mushroom soup

Combine bread cubes, onion, celery, seasonings, celery soup and milk; mix well. Refrigerate overnight or several hours. Next day mix beef with mustard and Worcestershire sauce. Toss raw meat mixture with dressing, mixing lightly. Spread into 13- x 9-in. pan. Spread mushroom soup over top. Bake at 350° about 1-1/2 hours.

Mrs. Marge Hennenfent, Cameron, Illinois

SQUAW CORN CASSEROLE

- **1 pound ground beef**
- **1/4 cup chopped onion**
- **1-1/2 teaspoons salt**
- **1/2 teaspoon thyme**
- **1/4 teaspoon marjoram**
- **2 eggs, beaten**
- **1/4 cup milk**
- **1 cup soft bread crumbs**
- **16-ounce can cream style corn**
- **2 teaspoons prepared mustard**
- **1/2 cup bread or cracker crumbs**

Brown beef and onions; drain fat. Add seasonings, eggs, milk, 1 cup soft crumbs, corn and mustard. Pour into greased casserole, top with 1/2 cup crumbs; bake at 350° 30-40 minutes. **Note:** Fresh or drained, canned tomatoes may be added to this recipe. Slice tomatoes and arrange in layers with beef mixture. *Mrs. Boneta Kerby, Glenwood, Missouri*

MOUSSAKA

- **1-1/2-pound eggplant**
- **6 cups boiling water**
- **1 pound ground beef**
- **1/2 cup chopped onion**
- **1 garlic clove, minced**
- **2 cups canned tomatoes**
- **1/2 cup chopped parsley**
- **1 teaspoon salt**
- **1/2 teaspoon cinnamon**
- **1/4 teaspoon nutmeg**
- **1/4 teaspoon pepper**
- **3 eggs**
- **1 teaspoon salt**
- **1/4 cup butter**
- **1/3 cup flour**
- **2 cups milk**
- **1 cup grated Parmesan cheese**

Peel and slice eggplant 1/2-in. thick. Cook in boiling salted (1 teaspoon) water, covered, about 5 minutes; drain. Brown beef, onion and garlic; drain fat. Add tomatoes, parsley, 1 teaspoon salt, cinnamon, nutmeg and pepper. Cook, uncovered, about 20 minutes, stirring occasionally until liquid evaporates. Meanwhile beat eggs and salt in small bowl. In medium saucepan melt butter, add flour, stirring until smooth. Remove from heat; stir in milk. Return to heat and cook, stirring until sauce thickens. Gradually stir 1/3 of hot sauce into eggs. Return to remaining sauce. Cook 1 minute, stirring. Remove from heat, stir in 3/4 cup Parmesan cheese. Remove meat sauce from heat, stir in 3/4 cup cream sauce. Arrange half of eggplant in 9-in. square, greased baking dish. Spread meat mixture over eggplant. Top with remaining eggplant. Pour remaining cream sauce over. Sprinkle with remaining 1/4 cup Parmesan cheese. Bake at 350° 30 minutes or until heated through. Let stand 10 minutes before serving.

Mrs. Angela Bunke, Winona, Minnesota

LAYERED OVERNIGHT CASSEROLE

- 4 fresh or 16-ounce can tomatoes
- 1 tablespoon butter
- 6-ounce package long grain and wild rice
- 1 pound ground beef
- 3/4 teaspoon salt
- 1/4 teaspoon pepper
- 2 cups shredded cabbage
- 1 tablespoon flour
- 1/2 to 1 cup sour cream
- 1 cup shredded cheddar cheese

Chop tomatoes. If using canned, drain, reserving juice. Add water to juice to make 2-1/2 cups. Add butter, rice and contents of seasoning packet to liquid. Bring to boil, reduce heat; cover and simmer about 25 minutes until rice is tender. Brown beef; drain fat. Add salt and pepper. Cover cabbage with boiling water, let stand 2 minutes; drain. Sprinkle with flour, toss to mix. Spread rice in 2-quart casserole. Layer cabbage, sour cream, ground beef, chopped tomatoes and cheese over rice. Cover and refrigerate overnight. Bake, uncovered, at 350° about 45 minutes or until hot.

Mrs. Meridith K. Snyder, Bringhurst, Indiana

GROUND BEEF STROGANOFF

- 1-1/2 pounds ground beef
- 1/4 cup chopped green pepper
- 1 envelope onion soup mix
- 3 tablespoons flour
- 2 tablespoons tomato paste
- 2-1/2 cups water
- 1 small can mushrooms, drained
- 1/2 cup dairy sour cream
- Cooked noodles
- Snipped parsley

Brown beef and green pepper. Blend in soup mix, flour and tomato paste. Stir in water. Cover and simmer 10 minutes. Stir in mushrooms and sour cream. Heat through—do not boil! Serve over cooked noodles. Garnish with parsley.

Carolyn Rubsam, Ocheyedan, Iowa

MACARONI RING HOT DISH

- 24 ounces large size macaroni rings, cooked
- 3 pounds ground beef
- 2 cups chopped onions
- 2 cups diced celery
- 1-1/2 teaspoons salt
- 1/4 teaspoon pepper
- 2 cans or jars spaghetti sauce with mushrooms
- 14-ounce bottle catsup
- 2 cans whole kernel corn
- 2 cans vegetable beef soup
- 3 tablespoons sugar

Cook macaroni just until tender—DO NOT OVERCOOK! Fry beef and onic until red color disappears; add celery, salt and pepper. Saute about 10 minutes. Place meat mixture in large roaster. Add the spaghetti sauce, catsup, corn, undiluted soup and sugar; mix to blend. Gently fold in macaroni rings, do not overstir to break the macaroni rings. Cover roaster and bake at 325° 1 hour. **Note**: This is a large recipe for a crowd.

Mrs. Fred Kraemer, Glencoe, Minnesota

GROUND BEEF POTATO CASSEROLE

1 pound ground beef
2 tablespoons butter
2 tablespoons flour
1/2 teaspoon seasoned salt
1 cup milk
2 ounces shredded processed cheese
4 medium-sized raw potatoes, shredded
1 medium-sized raw carrot, shredded
1 tablespoon chopped parsley

Brown beef; drain fat. Spread in bottom of 10- x 6-in. baking dish. Prepare white sauce by melting the butter, stir in flour. Slowly stir in milk until smooth, add salt. Cook over medium heat, stirring until sauce is thickened. Cook, stirring, 1 minute more. Stir in cheese until melted. Add potatoes and carrots; pour over meat. Cover with foil; bake at 350° 45 minutes. Uncover, sprinkle with parsley. Return to oven, bake 15 minutes longer. Serves 4 to 6.

Mrs. Loren W. Hurst, Milo, Iowa

ZUCCHINI CASSEROLE

4 cups zucchini
1 pound ground beef
1 cup chopped onion
1 teaspoon garlic salt
1 teaspoon salt
1 teaspoon basil
1/2 teaspoon oregano
1/4 teaspoon pepper
2 cups cooked rice
8 ounces tomato sauce
1 cup cottage cheese
1 egg, beaten
1 cup grated cheddar cheese

Cook sliced, unpeeled zucchini in small amount of boiling salted water about 4 minutes; drain well. Saute beef and onion. Add seasonings; drain fat. Add rice and tomato sauce to meat. Combine cottage cheese and egg. In 3-quart buttered baking dish layer half of zucchini. Spread meat mixture over squash, then cottage cheese mixture, then remaining zucchini. Sprinkle grated cheese over top. Bake, uncovered at 350° 40 to 50 minutes.

Mrs. Mary Ann Devney, Farmington, Minnesota

STUFFED CABBAGE ROLLS

12 large cabbage leaves
1-1/4 pounds ground beef
2 teaspoons salt
1/2 teaspoon pepper
1 cup cooked rice
1 onion, chopped
1 egg
1/2 teaspoon poultry seasoning

Sauce:

16 ounces tomato sauce
1 tablespoon brown sugar
1 tablespoon lemon juice OR vinegar
1/4 cup water

Cover cabbage leaves with boiling water; let stand 5 minutes; drain. Mix ground beef with remaining ingredients. Place equal amount of meat mixture on each cabbage leaf. Roll up folding edges in. Secure with wooden toothpicks, or tie with string. Place in greased skillet or baking dish. **Sauce:** Combine ingredients and pour over cabbage rolls. Cover and simmer 1 hour, or, if baking, bake at 350° 1 hour. *Carol Stinnett, Middle Point, Ohio*

NOODLE CASSEROLE

1-1/2 pounds ground beef
2 onions, chopped
Salt and pepper
2 small green pepper, chopped
1 can cream of tomato soup
6 ounces tomato paste
1 cup beef bouillon
16 ounces egg noodles
1 cup sour cream
1 cup sliced stuffed olives
1 cup mushrooms
Shredded cheese

Brown beef and onion; season to taste. Add green pepper, undiluted tomato soup, tomato paste and bouillon; simmer gently. Meanwhile cook noodles according to directions. Combine sour cream, olives and mushrooms. In large casserole dish, or 2 smaller ones, combine ingredients. Sprinkle tops with cheese; bake at 350° until bubbly, about 30 minutes.

Mrs. Becky Winans, Mt. Auburn, Illinois

BEEF BRUNCH SOUFFLE

1 pound ground beef
1-1/2 teaspoons seasoned salt
1/4 teaspoon nutmeg
6 eggs
1-1/2 cups milk
5 slices bread, cubed
1 cup shredded Swiss or sharp cheddar cheese
1 tablespoon diced pimiento

Brown beef, drain fat. Add seasoned salt and nutmeg; let cool. Beat eggs well; stir in milk then fold in bread cubes, cheese and pimiento. Stir in cooled ground beef. Spread mixture into greased 10- x 6-in. baking dish. Cover and refrigerate overnight. Bake at 325° 1 hour and 10 minutes. Let stand 5 minutes before cutting into squares. Serve immediately.

Mrs. Loren W. Hurst, Milo, Iowa

GROUND BEEF AND WILD RICE CASSEROLE

1 cup wild rice
4 cups boiling water
1 can cream of mushroom soup
1 can cream of chicken soup
8-ounce can sliced mushrooms
2 beef bouillon cubes
1 cup boiling water
1 bay leaf, crumbled
1/4 teaspoon EACH celery salt, garlic salt, pepper, onion salt and paprika
3/4 cup chopped celery
6 tablespoons chopped onion
2 tablespoons butter
1-1/2 to 2 pounds ground beef
1/2 cup slivered almonds

Pour boiling water over rice; let stand 15 minutes. Drain well; add soups, mushrooms and juice, bouillon cubes, dissolved in 1 cup boiling water, crumbled bay leaf and seasonings. Saute celery and onion in butter; add to rice mixture. Brown beef; drain fat. Add to rice. Pour into large greased baking dish; sprinkle with almonds. Cover and bake at 350° 1-1/2 hours or until rice is tender. Add more bouillon if rice becomes dry before done. **Note:** Recipe may be prepared day ahead. Refrigerated; baked next day. Allow an extra hour baking time.

Mrs. Paul Lenz, Ellsworth, Minnesota

SAVORY BOWKNOTS

1 pound ground beef
1/2 cup chopped green pepper
1 package dried onion soup mix
1 cup Burgundy wine
16 ounces tomato sauce
1/4 teaspoon pepper
1/4 cup chopped, fresh parsley
8 ounces egg bow noodles
1/2 cup grated Parmesan cheese

Saute beef and green pepper until meat is browned. Dissolve soup mix in wine; add to meat mixture with tomato sauce and pepper. Bring to boil, reduce heat and simmer, covered, 30 minutes. Stir in parsley. Cook noodles according to directions on package; drain well. Toss with meat sauce. Pour into 2-quart casserole dish, sprinkle with cheese; bake at 350° 15 minutes.

Charlotte Loveless, Sullivan, Indiana

CONFETTI CASSEROLE

2 pounds ground beef
1/2 cup chopped onion
2 teaspoons salt
1/4 teaspoon pepper
2 tablespoons brown sugar
8 ounces cream cheese
16-ounce can tomato sauce
20-ounce bag frozen mixed vegetables, defrosted

Brown meat and onion; salt and pepper to taste. Add sugar and cheese, stirring to melt cheese. Add tomato sauce and vegetables. Pour into greased 3-quart casserole; sprinkle with crushed corn or potato chips or bread crumbs. Cover and bake at 350° about 40 minutes. Uncover and bake 10 minutes more. *Thelma Meyer, Petersburg, North Dakota*

BEEF BARLEY CASSEROLE

4 slices bacon, diced
1 pound ground beef
2 cups chopped onion
2 cups chopped celery
1 can tomato soup
1 cup mushroom soup
2 teaspoons salt
1/4 cup pimiento or sweet red pepper
1 cup peas
1 cup uncooked pearl barley, soaked overnight
4 ounces mushrooms and juice

Brown bacon, beef and onion. Add remaining ingredients. Bake in large casserole dish at 350° 1 hour. *Mrs. Sidney Lorence, Racine, Wisconsin*

MAKE AHEAD CASSEROLE

1 pound ground beef
1/4 cup minced onion
1 clove garlic, minced
16 ounces tomato sauce
1 teaspoon salt
Dash pepper
1 cup dairy sour cream
1 cup cream style cottage cheese
1/4 cup chopped fresh parsley
1 cup sliced, cooked carrots
8 ounces medium noodles, cooked
1 cup shredded cheddar cheese

Brown beef, onion and garlic. Stir in tomato sauce, salt and pepper. Simmer, uncovered about 5 minutes. Combine sour cream, cottage cheese, parsley and cooked carrots. Add to cooked noodles; gently blend. Alternate layers of noodles and meat mixture in greased 3-quart casserole dish, beginning and ending with noodles. Top with cheddar cheese. Bake at 350° 30 to 45 minutes until hot and bubbly. *Mrs. Duane Muxen, Doland, South Dakota*

LAYERED HAMBURGER BAKE

- 10 ounces frozen, chopped spinach
- 3 cups dry noodles
- 1 pound ground beef
- 15 ounce can tomato sauce
- 1 teaspoon sugar
- 1/4 teaspoon garlic salt
- 1/8 teaspoon pepper
- 8 ounces cream cheese, softened
- 1/2 cup dairy sour cream
- 3 tablespoons milk
- 2 tablespoons chopped onion
- 1/2 cup shredded cheddar cheese

Cook spinach; drain well. Cook noodles; drain well. Brown beef in large skillet. Stir in tomato sauce, sugar, garlic salt, pepper and cooked noodles. Combine cream cheese and sour cream, milk and onion. In 13- x 9-in. baking dish, layer half of ground beef mixture, half of cream cheese mixture and all of spinach. Then layer remaining cheese mixture and meat mixture. Bake covered at 350° 40 minutes. Uncover, top with cheddar cheese and bake 10 minutes more.

Mrs. Barbara Larson, Castana, Iowa

SPICY MEAT STUFFED TOMATOES

- 6 large tomatoes
- 2-1/2 cups garlic and onion flavored croutons
- 3/4 cups water
- 2 tablespoons chopped parsley
- 1 teaspoon basil, crushed
- 1/2 teaspoon oregano, crushed
- 1/2 teaspoon thyme
- 1 pound ground beef
- 2 tablespoons butter
- 1/2 pound fresh mushrooms, finely chopped
- 1-1/2 teaspoons salt
- Dash pepper

Slice off tops of tomatoes. Carefully scoop out pulp to form shell, invert to drain. Crush croutons; reserve 1/3 cup. Combine remaining crumbs, water and herbs. Saute ground beef until browned; drain off fat. Add meat to crouton mixture. In same skillet, melt 1 tablespoon butter; add mushrooms and saute over medium heat until liquid evaporates and mushrooms brown. Add to meat mixture. Season with salt and pepper to taste. Spoon meat mixture into tomatoes; do not pack tightly but mound slightly. Melt remaining tablespoon butter, stir in crouton crumbs; sprinkle over tomatoes. Place in shallow baking dish and bake at 375° for 20 minutes.

Karla Boehs, Wilmore, Kansas

GRAVY GOODNESS: *Add leftover gravy to raw ground beef mixture for meat loaf; adds flavor and moisture.*

BEEF ROUNDUP

Dough:

3 cups flour
4 teaspoons baking powder
1 teaspoon salt
1/4 teaspoon marjoram
1/8 teaspoon sage
6 tablespoons shortening
1/2 cup tomato sauce
1/2 cup water

Filling:

2 pounds ground beef
3/4 cup minced onion
1/2 cup finely chopped celery
1 teaspoon salt
1/4 teaspoon pepper
4 ounces tomato sauce

Dough: Combine dry ingredients. Cut in shortening until mixture resembles coarse cornmeal. Add tomato sauce and water; mix. Turn dough onto floured board and knead 4 times. Roll to 13- x 9-in. rectangle. Place in 13- x 9-in. baking dish. **Filling**: Brown beef, onion and celery. Add remaining ingredients, reduce heat, cover and simmer until meat mixture is thickened, about 20 minutes. Spoon meat over dough. Bring sides up and pinch together. Bake at 350° about 35 minutes or until dough is golden.

Mrs. Harold Erboe, Westfield, Wisconsin

BEEFED-UP BISCUIT CASSEROLE

1 pound ground beef
1/2 cup chopped onion
1/4 cup diced green chiles OR green pepper
8 ounces tomato sauce
2 teaspoons chili powder, or to taste
1/2 teaspoon garlic salt
8-ounce can refrigerated buttermilk biscuits
1-1/2 cups shredded cheddar cheese, divided
1/2 cup sour cream
1 egg, slightly beaten

Brown beef, onion and peppers; drain fat. Stir in tomato sauce, chili powder and garlic salt. Simmer while preparing dough. Separate biscuit dough into 20 biscuits by pulling each biscuit apart. Press 10 biscuit layers over bottom of ungreased 8 or 9-in. square baking pan. Combine 1/2 cup shredded cheese, sour cream and egg; mix well. Remove meat mixture from stove; stir in sour cream mixture. Spoon over dough. Arrange remaining biscuits over top of meat, sprinkle with remaining cheese. Bake at 375° 25 to 30 minutes until biscuits are golden brown.

Barb Kalbach, Stuart, Iowa

STACK-A-ROLL STROGANOFF

1 pound ground beef
4 ounces mushrooms, drained
3-1/2 ounces French fried onions
10-1/2-ounce can cream of mushroom soup
1/2 cup dairy sour cream
9.5-ounce can refrigerator buttermilk biscuits

Topping:
1/2 cup sour cream
1 egg
1 teaspoon celery seed
1/2 teaspoon salt

Brown beef; drain fat. Combine beef, mushrooms and onion, reserving 1/2 cup onion for topping. Toss lightly, place in 2-1/2-quart casserole. Bring undiluted soup to boil, stir in sour cream. Pour warm soup mixture over meat. Separate dough into 10 biscuits. Cut each biscuit in half, forming 20 half circles. Arrange biscuits cut side down around edge of casserole. Sprinkle remaining onions in center. Combine topping ingredients; pour over biscuits. Bake at 375° 25-30 minutes until golden brown.

Mrs. Tom Hite, Ligonier, Indiana

MEAT 'N BISCUIT SQUARES

Rich Biscuit Dough:
2 cups flour
3 teaspoons baking powder
1 teaspoon salt
1/2 cup shortening
1 egg
1/2 cup milk

Filling:
1 pound ground beef
1/2 cup chopped onion
1 cup grated cheese
1 egg
1/4 teaspoon tabasco sauce
1-1/2 teaspoon salt
2 tablespoons chopped parsley
1 egg yoks, beaten

Filling: Saute beef and onion just until meat loses its color. Remove from heat; cool. Mix with cheese, egg, tabasco sauce, salt and parsley. **Biscuit dough**: Combine dry ingredients. Cut in shortening until mixture resembles coarse cornmeal. Stir in egg and milk. Turn onto floured board; knead lightly 15 times. Divide dough in half; roll into 9-in. square. Place in 9-in. square pan. Spread with meat mixture, cover with remaining dough rolled to 9-in. square. Brush top of dough with egg yolk. Bake at 400° about 30 minutes. Serve hot, cut in squares topped with hot tomato or mushroom soup.

Mrs. Harold Loberger, Oconto, Wisconsin

TOTE'M ROLLS

1 pound ground beef
1 envelope instant onion soup
3/4 teaspoon crushed oregano
1/8 teaspoon garlic salt
1/2 cup catsup
16 ounces refrigerated crescent rolls
1 cup shredded mozarella cheese
Poppy seeds

Brown ground beef, drain fat. Stir in soup mix, oregano, salt and catsup. Cool. Meanwhile separate crescent rolls into 8 rectangles. Seal perforations. Divide cooled hamburger mixture equally onto long side of each rectangle. Sprinkle with cheese. Roll up lengthwise, jelly roll fashion. Bring ends together to form a doughnut shape. Seal ends tightly. Brush tops with milk or melted butter, sprinkle with poppy seeds. Place rolls on ungreased baking sheet; bake at 375° for 15 minutes, or until golden brown. Makes 8 rolls. Serve hot or cold.

Sandra Lefever, Geneva, Nebraska

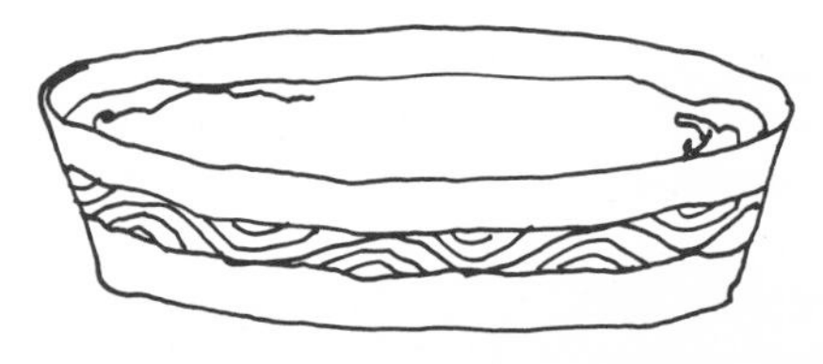

BEEFY CORN PIE

Crust:

1 pound ground beef
1/4 cup fine dry bread crumbs
1/4 cup catsup
2 tablespoons minced onion
1 teaspoon chili powder
1 teaspoon salt
1/2 teaspoon pepper

Topping:

1 egg
1/2 cup milk
8-1/2-ounce can creamed corn
16 ounces whole kernel corn, drained
2-1/2-ounce can sliced mushrooms, drained
1/3 cup chopped green pepper
1/4 teaspoon salt
3/4 cup shredded cheddar cheese

Crust: Combine ingredients; press into 9-in. square baking dish. **Topping:** Combine ingredients, except shredded cheese; pour over meat crust. Bake at 375° 35 to 45 minutes. Sprinkle cheese over top, bake 5 minutes more.

Kay L. Lehman, Manheim, Pennsylvania

MEAT LOAF PIE

1 pound ground beef
1 cup small curd cottage cheese
1 egg
1/2 cup quick cooking oatmeal
1/4 cup catsup
1 tablespoon prepared mustard
2 tablespoons chopped onion
3/4 teaspoon salt
1/4 teaspoon pepper
1/3 cup Parmesan cheese

Thoroughly mix all ingredients except Parmesan cheese. Pat into ungreased 9-in. pie pan. Bake at 350° 20 minutes. Sprinkle with Parmesan cheese and bake 10 minutes more. **Note:** Before serving, drain any fat that surfaces with poultry baster. *Mrs. Susan Phillips, Colorado Springs, Colorado*

HAMBURGER PIE

1 pound ground beef
1/2 cup chopped onion
1/2 teaspoon salt
Dash pepper
16 ounces cut green beans, drained
10-3/4-ounce can tomato soup
5 hot cooked potatoes
1/2 cup warm milk
1 egg, beaten
1/2 cup shredded American cheese

Brown beef and onion; season with salt and pepper. Add beans and soup; pour into 1-1/2 quart casserole. Mash hot potatoes with milk and egg. Spoon in mounds over meat mixture. Sprinkle potatoes with cheese. Bake at 350° 25 minutes. *Annette Dubas, Palmer, Nebraska*

BEEF BROCCOLI PIE

1 pound ground beef
10-ounce package frozen chopped broccoli
2 tablespoons flour
1-1/4 cups milk
1/2 tablespoon minced onion
3/4 teaspoon salt
1/4 teaspoon garlic salt
1 egg
3-ounce package cream cheese
Slices of cheese, Monterey Jack OR cheddar
1 package crescent rolls

Saute beef until browned. Cook broccoli until just tender; drain. Mix flour, milk, onion, salts, egg and cheese in blender or mixer until smooth. Combine beef, broccoli and cheese sauce; spread in greased 9-in. square baking dish. Cover mixture with slices of cheese. Use either Italian crescent rolls or plain. Unroll dough and cover cheese to form crust. Bake at 350° 40 minutes. Let stand 10 minutes before serving. *Mrs. Ken Landes, Wooster, Ohio*

AMERICAN PIECE-A-PIE

Crust:

- 1 cake compressed yeast
- 1/4 cup lukewarm water
- 1 egg
- 1/4 cup tomato sauce
- 1 tablespoon sugar
- 3 tablespoons melted shortening
- 1 teaspoon salt
- 1/2 teaspoon chili powder
- 2 to 2-1/4 cups flour

Hamburger Topping:

- 1/2 pound ground beef
- 1/4 cup chopped onion
- 3/4 cup tomato sauce
- 1/2 teaspoon chili powder
- 1/2 teaspoon salt
- Dash pepper
- 2 cups shredded American cheese

Crust: Soften yeast in warm water in large bowl. Add egg, tomato sauce, sugar, shortening, salt and chili powder; blend well. Add flour gradually, blending after each addition. Knead on lightly floured board until smooth and satiny. Place in greased bowl, cover and let rise until doubled in bulk, about 1 hour. Meanwhile prepare topping. Brown beef and onion. Add tomato sauce and seasonings. Pat or roll out dough on greased 15- x 11-in. baking sheet to within 1/2 inch of edge of sheet. Brush with 2 tablespoons melted butter. Spread with meat filling, sprinkle with shredded cheese. Bake at 425° 15 to 18 minutes.

Mrs. Henry Binkley, Bois D'Arc, Missouri

CHEESEBURGER PIE

- 9-in. unbaked pie shell
- 1 pound ground beef
- 1/4 cup chopped onion
- 1/2 teaspoon oregano
- 1 teaspoon salt
- 1/4 teaspoon pepper
- 1/2 cup fine dry bread crumbs
- 8 ounces tomato sauce

Cheese topping:

- 8 ounces cheddar cheese, shredded
- 1 egg, beaten
- 1/4 cup milk
- 1/2 teaspoon each salt, dry mustard, Worcestershire sauce

Brown beef and onion; drain fat. Combine seasonings and crumbs. Add to meat along with tomato sauce. Spread in prepared pie shell. Combine cheese topping ingredients; spread over meat filling. Bake at 425° 30 minutes.

Mrs. Sharon Rolston, Jamestown, Indiana

HAMBURGER SPUD PIE

Crust:

1/2 cup instant potato flakes, divided
2 tablespoons melted butter
2 cups flour
1 tablespoon sugar
1 teaspoon cream of tartar
1 teaspoon baking soda
1/3 cup butter
1/2 cup milk
1/4 cup mayonnaise
1/2 cup shredded cheese

Filling:

1 pound ground beef
1/2 cup chopped onion
1 teaspoon salt
1/4 teaspoon pepper
3/4 cup instant potato flakes
1 egg
1/4 cup catsup
1/4 cup hamburger relish
1 tablespoon prepared mustard

Crust: Combine 1/4 cup potato flakes with melted butter; set aside. Combine 1/4 cup potato flakes and dry ingredients. Cut in butter, add milk, cheese and mayonnaise to make soft dough. Roll or pat into bottom and sides of large pie plate. **Filling:** Brown beef and onion; add remaining ingredients, mixing well. Spread over crust; sprinkle potato, butter crumbs over top. Bake at 350° till crust is golden brown and meat mixture is done.

Mrs. Rita Nunn, GAFB, Montana

HAMBURGER ONION PIE

1 cup Bisquick
1/3 cup light cream
1 pound ground beef
2 medium-sized onions, thinly sliced
1 teaspoon salt
1/4 teaspoon pepper
1/2 teaspoon flavor extender (MSG)
2 tablespoons Bisquick
2 eggs
1 cup small curd cottage cheese
Paprika

Mix 1 cup Bisquick and cream. Knead 10 times on board that's lightly dusted with Bisquick. Roll dough to fit 9-in. pie pan. Ease into pan, press around edge of dough with tines of fork. Saute beef until lightly browned. Remove from skillet with slotted spoon. Saute onions in beef drippings until soft, but not browned; drain fat. Combine beef, onions, seasonings and 2 tablespoons Bisquick; spread over crust. Beat eggs, blend in cottage cheese; pour over meat. Sprinkle top with paprika. Bake at 375° 30 minutes.

Donna Stangler, Owatonna, Minnesota

BEEF AND GREEN BEAN PIE

- 1-1/4 pounds ground beef
- 1/3 cup chopped onion
- 8 ounces tomato sauce with mushrooms
- 16-ounce can green beans, drained
- Salt and pepper to taste
- 1 tube crescent refrigerator rolls
- 1 egg, slightly beaten
- 2 cups shredded Monterey Jack OR cheddar cheese, divided

Brown beef and onion; drain fat. Stir in tomato sauce and green beans; simmer while preparing crust. Separate rolls and press into 9-in. pie pan; cover bottom and sides well. Combine beaten egg and 1 cup cheese; spread over crust. Spoon hot meat mixture into crust. Sprinkle with remaining cheese. Bake at 350° 25 minutes. Let stand 5 minutes before cutting into wedges.

Mrs. John McCann, Ames, Iowa

COMPANY SKILLET DINNER

- 1 egg, slightly beaten
- 1/2 cup milk
- 2 tablespoons wheat germ
- 2 slices bread, diced
- 1/2 teaspoon nutmeg
- 1/4 teaspoon pepper
- 1/2 teaspoon celery salt
- 1 teaspoon dry mustard
- 1 medium-sized onion, finely chopped
- 1 pound ground beef
- 3 tablespoons butter
- 1/2 cup sliced fresh mushrooms
- 2 tablespoons butter
- 1 can cream of mushroom soup
- 1/2 cup milk
- 1/4 cup cooking wine (Sherry)
- 1-pound can green beans, drained

In bowl combine egg, milk, wheat germ and bread. Add spices, onion and meat; mix well. Shape into 1-in. balls; roll in flour. Melt 3 tablespoons butter in deep skillet; brown meatballs on all sides. Remove to warm platter; keep warm. Into the skillet, add mushrooms and 2 tablespoons butter; saute lightly. Stir in undiluted soup, milk and cooking wine. Simmer 3 minutes; add meatballs and green beans. Simmer about 10 minutes longer to heat through.

Helen Haaland, Woodbury, Connecticut

BOUNTY HAMBURGER RICE SKILLET

1 pound ground beef
16-ounce can tomatoes
1 tablespoon salt
1/2 teaspoon each oregano, basil and garlic powder
3 cups cooked rice
4 cups cabbage, coarsely shredded
1/2 cup sour cream
1 cup each finely chopped onions and green peppers
1 cup grated mozzarella cheese

Saute beef until lightly browned. Stir in tomatoes, seasonings, rice and cabbage. Cover and cook 10 to 15 minutes or until cabbage is tender crisp. Stir in sour cream, onions and green pepper. **Note:** Saute onion and green pepper with beef, if desired. Heat. Spoon into warm serving dish and sprinkle with cheese. Let stand a few minutes before serving to allow cheese to melt. Yield: 6 to 8 servings.

Rice Council of America

BEEF AND SAUERKRAUT SKILLET

1 pound ground beef
1 cup chopped onion
1-1/2 teaspoons salt
1/4 teaspoon pepper
1 cup uncooked rice (not instant)
1-pound can sauerkraut
16 ounces tomato sauce
1/4 cup water

Brown beef and onion in skillet. Stir in remaining ingredients. Cover and simmer about 35 minutes or until rice is tender.

Mrs. William Burr, Bird City, Kansas

SKILLET MEAL

1 pound ground beef
1 medium sized onion
1/4 cup butter
16 ounces tomatoes and juice
1 tablespoon Worcestershire sauce
1-1/2 cups uncooked noodles
3/4 cup frozen mixed vegetables
2-1/4-ounce can sliced ripe olives, optional
Salt and pepper to taste
4 ounces American cheese, shredded

Saute beef and onion in melted butter. Add tomatoes, Worcestershire sauce, noodles, vegetables and olives. Salt and pepper to taste. Bring mixture to boil, reduce to medium heat, cover and let mixture simmer 30 minutes, stirring frequently. Sprinkle cheese over top, cover and cook 5 minutes more to melt cheese.

Mrs. JoAnn Abbott, Miles City, Montana

ZUCCHINI BEEF SKILLET

- 1 pound ground beef
- 1 cup chopped onion
- 3/4 cup chopped green pepper
- 1-1/2 teaspoons salt
- 1/4 teaspoon pepper
- 1 teaspoon chili powder, optional
- 5 cups sliced zucchini
- 2 large tomatoes, chopped
- 1-1/4 cups whole kernel corn
- 2 tablespoons chopped pimientos
- 1/4 cup chopped fresh parsley

Brown beef, onion and green pepper. Add remaining ingredients, except parsley. Cover and simmer 10 to 15 minutes until vegetables are tender crisp. Garnish with parsley.

Mrs. Lois Garber, Lancaster, Pennsylvania

QUICK SKILLET DINNER

- 1 pound ground beef
- Salt and pepper
- 1 teaspoon Worcestershire sauce
- 2 16-ounce cans mixed vegetables
- 1 small can tomato paste
- 2 cups mashed potatoes
- 1/2 cup shredded cheddar cheese
- Paprika

Brown beef, season to taste; stir in Worcestershire sauce. Add drained vegetables and tomato paste. Heat thoroughly, stirring occasionally. Prepare mashed potatoes, drop by spoonfuls around edge of skillet. Sprinkle with cheese and dust with paprika. Place in hot oven to melt cheese.

Mrs. Clarissa T. Percival, Weeks Mills, Maine

TOASTY TOPPING: *Save those leftover, untouched pieces of toast. Cut into cubes and store in airtight container. Mix cubes with grated cheese, dry onion soup mix or saute lightly in bacon grease. They're great for casseroles or salads.*

Mrs. Walter Peterson, Watertown, Wisconsin.

CHIP TOP: *Don't discard those broken crumbs of potato chips in the bottom of the bag! Save them for casserole toppings!*

Mrs. Orlin Petersen, Utica, South Dakota

Chili, Soups and Stews

CHILI

4 pounds ground beef
8 medium-sized onions, chopped
4 1-pound 12-ounce cans whole tomatoes
4 15-1/2-ounce cans kidney or red beans
1 large can tomato paste
2 tablespoons sugar
3 tablespoons chili powder
1 tablespoon plus 1-1/2 teaspoons salt

Brown beef and onions in very large pan. Add tomatoes, juice from beans, tomato paste, spices and sugar. Bring to boil; reduce heat, simmer 1-1/2 hours. Add beans, cook 20 minutes more. Serves 25.

Mrs. Diane Churchill, St. Louis Park, Minnesota

CHILI SOUP FOR A CROWD

14 pounds ground beef
4 large onions, chopped
3 green peppers, chopped
3 quarts whole tomatoes
5 quarts tomato juice
8 8-ounce cans tomato sauce
7 1-pound, 15-ounce cans Mexican style beans in chili gravy
6 tablespoons chili powder (or to taste)
5 bay leaves

Brown beef, onions and pepper; drain fat. In your large canning kettle, combine all ingredients. Bring to boil, reduce heat and simmer 4 or 5 hours. If you prefer kidney beans, drain them; add more tomato juice to soup, and more chili powder to taste. Serves 40. *Mrs. Elmer Strahm, Sabetha, Kansas*

CHILIGETTI

1 pound ground beef
1 onion, chopped
1 clove garlic, minced
2-1/2 cups tomatoes
8-ounce package spaghetti
3 cups shredded cheddar cheese
1/4 cup brown sugar
2 teaspoons salt
1 teaspoon chili powder
2 15-ounce cans chili with beans
1 cup Parmesan cheese

Brown beef, onion and garlic; drain fat. Add tomatoes, simmer 45 minutes. Cook spaghetti as directed on package; drain. Fold cheddar cheese into meat mixture; stir to melt cheese. Add spaghetti, sugar, salt, chili powder and chili with beans. Pour into 13- x 9-in. casserole dish. Sprinkle Parmesan cheese over top. Bake at 350° 45 minutes.

Mrs. Judith Voelker, Brownsdale, Minnesota

CHILI BAKE

1 pound ground beef
1 onion, chopped
1 green pepper, chopped
2-1/2 cups canned tomatoes
1-pound can kidney beans
1-1/2 teaspoons chili powder
2 teaspoons salt
Dash pepper

Tangy Muffins:

1 cup flour
1-1/2 teaspoons baking powder
1/2 teaspoon salt
1/2 teaspoon dry mustard
1 egg, beaten
1/2 cup milk
1 tablespoon melted shortening

Brown beef and onion; add remaining meat ingredients. Simmer gently while preparing Tangy Muffins: Combine dry ingredients. Combine egg, milk and shortening. Add to dry ingredients, stirring only until flour is moistened. Drop by spoonfuls on chili mixture. Cover tightly; simmer slowly 25 minutes. Do not remove cover until time is up.

Mrs. George L. Ott, Reeder, North Dakota

MEATBALL CHOWDER

2 pounds ground beef
2 teaspoons seasoned salt
1/8 teaspoon pepper
2 eggs, slightly beaten
1/4 cup chopped parsley
1/3 cup fine cracker crumbs
2 tablespoons milk
3 tablespoons flour
1 tablespoon salad oil
4 to 6 onions, cut into 8ths
6 cups water
6 cups tomato juice
6 beef bouillon cubes
6 carrots, sliced
4 cups sliced celery
3 potatoes, diced
1/4 cup long grain rice
1 tablespoon sugar
2 teaspoons salt
2 bay leaves
1/2 teaspoon marjoram
12 ounces canned Mexicorn

Combine meat, salt, pepper, eggs, parsley, crumbs and milk. Mix thoroughly. Form into walnut-size balls. Roll in flour; brown in hot oil. In soup pot bring remaining ingredients to a boil (except corn). Add meatballs then corn. Reduce heat; simmer until vegetables are tender. Yield 6 to 7 quarts.

Mrs. Johnny Flom, Dennison, Minnesota

BEAN BEEF SOUP

2 cups soup beans (1/2 cup soybeans, 1/2 cup red beans and 1 cup horticultural beans)
1/2 cup chopped onions
1/4 teaspoon garlic salt
1/2 cup sliced carrots
1/2 cup chopped celery
1 pound ground beef
1 egg
1/4 cup minced onion
1/4 cup bread crumbs
2 tablespoons minced parsley
1/8 teaspoon thyme
1/8 teaspoon marjoram

Soak beans in water overnight. Cook beans in water 1 hour, adding water as needed. Add 1/2 cup onions and garlic; cook 1 hour. Add carrots and celery; simmer 30 minutes. Mix beef, egg, onion crumbs, parsley and spices. Shape into balls; brown on all sides. Add to soup; simmer 25 minutes. Serves 6 to 8.

Mrs. Leroy S. Ulin, Sigourney, Iowa

HAMBURGER VEGETABLE SOUP WITH DUMPLINGS

1 pound ground beef
1 cup chopped onions
1 cup diced potatoes
1 cup sliced carrots
5 cups beef stock OR bouillon
4 cups canned tomatoes
1/4 cup rice OR barley
1 cup shredded cabbage
1 cup sliced celery
Salt to taste
1/4 teaspoon basil
1/4 teaspoon thyme
1 bay leaf

Dumplings:
2 eggs, well beaten
2/3 cup milk
1/2 teaspoon salt
2 cups flour (approximately)

Saute the ground beef and onion until lightly browned. Drain off fat, add remaining soup ingredients. Bring to boil, cover and simmer 1 hour. **Dumplings:** Combine eggs, milk, salt and enough flour to make soft dough. Drop by half teaspoonfuls into simmering soup. Keep soup simmering, cook dumplings until done, about 8 to 10 minutes.

Mrs. Gerald Mertz, Thomasboro, Illinois

CURE FOR ONION TEARS: *Peel and slice onions on top of your stove with the hood fan in operation. You'll do the job without a tear.*

Mrs. Helmer Olsen, Hayti, South Dakota

VALLEY OF THE SUN SOUP

1/2 pound ground beef
1/2 cup cooked rice
1/4 cup chopped celery
1/4 cup chopped onion
1/2 teaspoon ground cumin
1/2 teaspoon chili powder
1 can tomato soup
1 can bean with bacon soup
1-1/2 soup can water
Salt and pepper to taste

Brown beef; add remaining ingredients. Heat through; serve.

Mrs. Arthur Dole, Garfield, Washington

"SCUSE ME" BEAN HOTDISH

1 pound ground beef
1/2 cup chopped onion
1/2 teaspoon salt
1/4 teaspoon black pepper
1/2 cup catsup
2 tablespoons vinegar
1/4 teaspoon hot pepper sauce (tabasco)
1 tablespoon Worcestershire sauce
2 tablespoons brown sugar
16-ounce can pork and beans

Brown beef and onion, salt and pepper. Drain off fat. Add remaining ingredients. Pour into 1-1/2-quart casserole dish; bake at 350° 45 minutes.

Sandra Johnson, Leeds, North Dakota

CALICO BEANS

2 pounds ground beef
1/2 pound bacon
1 large onion, chopped
1/2 cup catsup
1 teaspoon dry mustard
1 teaspoon salt
Pepper to taste
2 teaspoons vinegar
1 tablespoon brown sugar
16-ounce can pork and beans
16-ounce can lima beans, drained
16-ounce can red kidney beans, drained

Dice bacon; saute until crisp. Remove with slotted spoon; set aside. Brown ground beef and onion in bacon fat; drain off fat. Add catsup, mustard, salt, pepper, vinegar and brown sugar; stir. Add bacon and beans. Pour into large baking casserole. Bake at 350° about 1 hour.

Mrs. Wilmont Pauling, Granville, Iowa

SQUASH STEW

- 1 pound ground beef
- 1 large onion, chopped
- 2 green peppers, chopped
- 6 medium-sized potatoes, peeled, diced
- 6 medium-sized tomatoes, chopped
- 1 pound green beans, fresh or frozen
- 2 large zucchini squash, peeled, cut in 1-in. chunks
- 2 large summer squash, peeled, cut in 1-in. chunks
- 1 tablespoon salt
- 1 tablespoon garlic salt
- 1 teaspoon basil
- 1 teaspoon oregano
- Pepper to taste

Brown beef, onion and green pepper in large stock pot. Add remaining ingredients; cover and simmer 1 hour, stirring occasionally.

Mrs. Carol C. Allen, Rodman, New York

HOBO STEW

- 2 pounds ground beef
- 1 cup thinly sliced onion
- 1 cup chopped green pepper
- 16 ounces kidney beans
- 16 ounces whole kernel corn
- 16 ounces tomato sauce
- 32-ounce can tomatoes
- 1 tablespoon steak sauce
- Basil, dry mustard, salt and pepper to taste

Brown beef, onion and green pepper. Add remaining ingredients; simmer gently about 30 minutes. *Mrs. Vernon Coe, Sr., Windham, New York*

WITCHES BREW

- 1/4 pound bacon, diced
- 1-1/2 pounds ground beef
- 1 green pepper, diced
- 1 large onion, diced
- 1 stalk celery, diced
- 1 quart canned tomatoes with juice
- 16-ounce can kidney beans, drained
- 4-ounce can chopped mushrooms
- 2 cups uncooked spaghetti rings
- Salt and pepper to taste
- 1 cup grated cheddar cheese

Fry bacon crisp; remove and drain on paper toweling. In bacon grease, saute onion, green pepper and celery until tender but not brown. Remove with slotted spoon. Brown beef; drain fat. Combine bacon, vegetables, beef and remaining ingredients except cheese. Place in large casserole dish; sprinkle with cheese. Bake at 350° 1 hour or until spaghetti rings are done.

Gloria Knipp, Tipton, Missouri

HOMESTEAD SKILLET STEW

2 pounds ground beef
1/4 cup chopped onion
1 egg
1/4 cup bread crumbs
1/2 cup tomato sauce
Salt and pepper to taste
1 large onion
6 carrots, cut in chunks
4 potatoes, quartered
2 cups green beans
1-1/2 cups water
16 ounces tomato sauce

Combine beef, 1/4 cup onion, egg, bread crumbs, 1/2 cup tomato sauce (taken from the 16 ounces) salt and pepper. Shape into meatballs or patties; brown in small amount of oil. Drain fat. Add remaining ingredients. Cover and simmer 1 hour. Thicken with a tablespoon or 2 of flour if sauce is too thin. **Note:** Vary the vegetables in this stew to your liking or to your garden harvest. *Gail M. Halverson, Cottage Grove, Minnesota*

BITS O'BACON: *Slice 1/2-in. strip off each end of a new package of bacon. Store in plastic bag in refrigerator or freezer. Pieces are ready for salad or casserole toppings.* *Mrs. Keith Herrman, Connell, Washington*

HAMBURGER STRETCHER: *Mix 1-1/2 cups poultry dressing with 1 pound ground beef. Add a little milk. Nice flavor change and meat stretcher.* *Mrs. Jim Pate, Williamston, North Carolina*

EASE THE CHEESE: *Some cheese toughens if baked too long. To prevent this, add grated cheese toppings to baked casseroles just a few minutes before removing from oven to melt cheese.* *Mrs. Mildred Sherrer, Bay City, Texas*

PIE CRUST WITH A DIFFERENCE: *For a flaky pie crust, combine 2 cups Bisquick Mix and 1/2 cup whipping cream. Work as you would any other pie dough.* *Mrs. Lloyd Henke, Owatonna, Minnesota*

FLAVOR FRIEND: *Use beef or chicken bouillon cubes to heighten the flavor in gravies, soups and stews. Add a cube to creamed sauces for zest; it will transform a vegetable dish.* *Mrs. Kathryn M. Wilson, Pontiac, Michigan*

Hamburgers

STUFFED BURGER BUNDLES

Stuffing:

1 box Stove Top chicken-flavored dressing mix
1/2 cup plus 2 tablespoons water
1 tablespoon butter
1 tablespoon plus 1 teaspoon vegetable seasoning packet
1 cup stuffing crumbs
1/3 cup quick cooking oatmeal
1/3 cup milk

Hamburgers:

1 pound ground beef
1/2 teaspoon salt
1/8 teaspoon pepper
1/4 cup finely diced onion

Sauce:

1 can cream of mushroom soup
2 tablespoons Worcestershire sauce

Stuffing: Heat water with butter and vegetable seasoning. Boil gently 5 minutes. Add 1 cup stuffing crumbs; stir to mix. Cover and let stand to cool. Mix oatmeal with milk; let stand 5 minutes; stir into stuffing mixture. **Hamburger:** Combine ingredients; divide into 4 equal portions. Shape each portion into large pattie. Divide the stuffing mix evenly placing in the center of each pattie. Bring meat up and around to enclose stuffing. Do not pull meat too tight to break pattie. Place patties in single layer in baking dish. **Sauce:** Mix soup with Worcestershire sauce; pour over patties. Bake, uncovered at 325° 45 to 50 minutes.

Mrs. Fred Kraemer, Glencoe, Minnesota

SALISBURY STEAK

10-3/4-ounce can cream of mushroom soup
2 teaspoons prepared mustard
2 teaspoons Worcestershire sauce
1 teaspoon horseradish
1-1/2 pounds ground beef
1 egg, slightly beaten
1/4 cup fine dry bread crumbs
1/4 cup finely chopped onion
1/2 teaspoon salt
Dash pepper
1/2 cup water
2 tablespoons chopped parsley

Blend soup, mustard, Worcestershire sauce and horseradish. Combine beef, 1/4 cup soup mixture, egg, crumbs, onion and seasonings. Shape into 6 large patties. Brown patties in skillet; drain fat. Add remaining soup mixture, water and parsley. Cover; cook over low heat 20 minutes.

Mrs. Jeannette Schwaegler, Burley, Idaho

GROUND ROUND SURPRISE

1 pound ground round steak
1/2 pound ground beef
1 cup shredded cheddar cheese
4 slices bacon, diced
2 tablespoons Worcestershire sauce
1 teaspoon salt
Dash pepper
1 egg
1/2 teaspoon celery salt
2 tablespoons catsup

Mix ingredients well; shape into patties of desired size. Grill patties on outdoor grill or broil in oven to desired doneness. Or meat mixture may be formed into a loaf and baked at 350° about 1 hour.

Mrs. Rudolf Riessen, Hartley, Iowa

CHOW MEIN BURGERS

3 pounds ground beef
1 egg, beaten
1/2 cup soy sauce
1/2 teaspoon pepper
1/2 cup mushrooms, canned or fresh
1-1/2 cups chopped onion, or to taste
1-1/2 cups bean sprouts, chopped
1-1/2 cups chow mein noodles
Hamburger rolls

Combine ingredients, mix well and shape into patties. Grill over hot, gray coals until patties are cooked to desired doneness. Toast rolls during last minutes before burgers are done. Serves 6 to 8.

Pat Stoebner, Tripp, South Dakota

YUMMY BURGERS

1-1/2 pounds ground beef
1 egg
1/4 cup finely chopped onion
1/2 cup cracker crumbs
2 tablespoons creamy French dressing
2 tablespoons grated Parmesan cheese
1/4 teaspoon salt
1/4 cup creamy French salad dressing
6 hamburger buns

In bowl beat egg; add onion, cracker crumbs, 2 tablespoons dressing, cheese and salt; mix well. Add meat and mix thoroughly. Shape into 6 patties. Grill or broil patties, basting with 1/4 cup dressing until done to your liking. Serve on toasted, buttered buns.

Mrs. Roger Reed, Des Moines, Iowa

BEEF PATTIES PARMESAN

1 pound ground beef
1/2 cup Bisquick mix
1/3 cup tomato juice
1/4 cup finely chopped green pepper
1 egg, slightly beaten
1 clove garlic, minced
1 teaspoon salt
1/2 teaspoon oregano
Dash pepper
1/2 teaspoon Worcestershire sauce
3 tablespoons grated Parmesan cheese
Buttered noodles OR Spanish rice

In bowl, combine all ingredients except cheese and noodles; mix well. Shape into 4 patties. Place in greased shallow baking pan. Bake at 400° 20 minute or until patties are done to your liking. Sprinkle with cheese and serve over buttered, hot noodles or Spanish rice.

Mrs. Christina Swope, Warrensburg, Illinois

MOCK CHICKEN FRIED STEAK

1 pound ground beef
2 teaspoons dried onion flakes
2 teaspoons parsley flakes
1 egg
1 teaspoon salt
1 tablespoon chili powder, or to taste
2 cups cracker crumbs
1/4 cup wheat germ

Mix beef, onion and parsley flakes, chili powder, egg, salt and half of cracker crumbs and wheat germ. Divide mixture into meat patties, the size you desire. Combine remaining cracker crumbs and wheat germ. Dip patties in crumb mixture, coating each side. Chill 30 minutes. Fry in hot oil, browning well on both sides.

Mrs. Elizabeth McJunkin, Toronto, Kansas

MOO BURGERS

1-1/2 pounds ground beef
1 cup sour cream
2 tablespoons Worcestershire sauce
2 tablespoons chopped onion
1-1/2 teaspoons salt
1-1/2 cups cornflakes

Combine meat, sour cream, Worcestershire sauce, onion and salt. Crush cornflakes slightly with your hands. Stir into meat mixture; shape into 8 patties, 3/4-in. thick. Broil about 5 minutes on each side, or until done to your liking. Patties may be cooked in skillet on stove top burner for approximately the same time.

Mrs. Roy Tempel, Higginsville, Missouri

GRILLED STUFFED HAMBURGERS

1 pound ground beef
Shredded cheese
Finely chopped onions
Drained pickle relish

Divide meat into 6 portions. Shape into ball; place on sheet of waxed paper far enough apart to roll thin. Place second sheet of waxed paper over meat. Roll into thin, large patties. Sprinkle 3 patties with cheese, onion and pickle relish. Cover with remaining 3 patties. Seal edges well with fingers. Place on greased grill; cook patties to your liking. Yield: 3 hamburgers.

Janet Petersen, Utica, South Dakota

MEAT FILLETS

2 pounds ground beef
1 cup applesauce
1 tablespoon chopped onion
1/4 cup chopped pimiento
1/2 cup dry oatmeal
1 cup ground carrots
2 eggs
2 teaspoons salt
1/4 teaspoon pepper
Bacon slices

Combine ingredients, except bacon slices; mix well. Shape meat into large patties. Wrap slice of bacon around edge of each pattie; secure ends with wooden toothpick. Arrange in shallow baking pan. Bake at 350° about 1 hour or until meat is done to your liking.

Mrs. Marsha Akerson, Aurora, Nebraska

BACON WRAPPED BEEF PATTIES

1 pound ground beef
1/2 cup shredded cheddar cheese
1/3 cup chopped onion
2 tablespoons catsup
1 tablespoon grated Parmesan cheese
1 tablespoon Worcestershire sauce
1/2 teaspoon salt
Dash pepper
1 egg
6 slices bacon

Combine beef with remaining ingredients, except bacon. Mix well. Shape into 11-in. roll. Lay bacon slices flat on sheet of waxed paper large enough to hold beef roll. Roll bacon around beef roll, securing ends of bacon with wooden toothpicks. Cut roll between bacon strips. Place the 6 bacon wrapped patties on broiler pan. Broil 7-in. from broiler for 6 minutes on first side, 3 minutes on the other. Or broil to your desired degree of doneness.

Mrs. Randy Koehl, Hancock, Minnesota

MUSHROOM STEAK

4 pounds ground beef
1/2 cup quick cooking oatmeal
1-1/2 cups milk
1 egg
1-3/4 teaspoons salt
Pepper to taste
Garlic salt, optional
1 tablespoon Worcestershire sauce
Cracker crumbs and flour

Gravy:
1 cup finely chopped celery
1 onion, chopped
1 green pepper, chopped
1 can cream of mushroom soup
1 cup water
2 cups tomato juice
2 cans sliced mushrooms (use liquid for part of water)

Mix beef, oatmeal, milk, egg, seasonings and Worcestershire sauce as for meat loaf. Shape portions into oval shape, size you desire. Pat into the cracker crumb and flour mixture to coat well on each side. Allow steaks to stand about 30 minutes to set coating. Brown steaks in greased hot skillet. Place meat in large roaster, cover with combined gravy ingredients. Cover roaster and bake at 300° about 1-1/2 hours.

Mrs. Kenneth D. Schrock, Congerville, Illinois

ARMENIAN "SLOPPY JOES" IN POCKET BREAD

4-6 flat bread rounds (Pita bread)
2 tablespoons cooking oil
1 pound ground beef
1 medium onion, chopped
1 or 2 cloves garlic, minced
1/2 cup regular wheat germ
1/2 cup chopped celery
1/2 cup minced parsley
1 teaspoon dried mint leaves, crushed (optional)
1/2-1 teaspoon oregano, crushed
3/4 teaspoon salt
1-1-1/2 cups dairy sour cream
Chopped tomatoes
Shredded lettuce
Thinly sliced cucumber

Saute beef, onion and garlic in hot oil. Add wheat germ, celery, parsley, mint and seasonings. Cook and stir several minutes. Add sour cream; cook over low heat until mixture is hot, stirring occasionally. Meanwhile wrap bread in foil. Heat at 350° 10 to 15 minutes. Cut bread rounds in half (from top to bottom not horizontally). Spoon meat mixture into slit in bread. Serve with remaining sour cream, lettuce, tomatoes piled into pockets.

Mrs. Earl Richabaugh, Shreve, Ohio

SUPPER ON FRENCH BREAD

- 1-1/2 pounds ground beef
- 2/3 cup undiluted evaporated milk
- 1/2 cup cracker or bread crumbs
- 1 egg
- 1/2 cup chopped onion
- 1 tablespoon prepared mustard
- 1-1/2 teaspoons salt
- 1/8 teaspoon pepper
- 3/4 teaspoon Accent seasoning (MSG)
- 2 cups grated American cheese
- 1 loaf French bread

Combine beef with remaining ingredients, except French bread; mix well. Cut bread in half lengthwise. Reserve top half for serving at another meal. Spread meat mixture over bottom half of bread. Place bread on foil shaping foil around sides of bread, but do not cover top filling. Place on cookie sheet; bake at 350° 25 minutes or until meat is done. Garnish with strips of cheese; bake 5 minutes more. To serve, cut into slices.

Mrs. Louis J. Easi, Sr., Streator, Illinois

BAR-B-Q'S

- 1 pound ground beef
- 1 or 2 onions, chopped
- 2 tablespoons flour
- 1/2 cup water
- 12-ounce bottle chili sauce
- 1/4 cup brown sugar
- 1 tablespoon vinegar
- Salt, pepper and chili powder to taste
- 12-ounce can corned beef
- Hamburger buns

Brown beef and onions. Stir in flour. Add water, chili sauce, brown sugar and vinegar. Season to taste with salt, pepper and chili powder. Dice or break up corned beef, add to beef mixture. Simmer for 1 hour. Serve on buns.

Janie Stevens, Sturgis, Michigan

BEEF SANDWICH FILLING

- 1 pound ground beef
- 1 or 2 hard cooked eggs, chopped
- 1/4 cup diced celery
- 3 tablespoons pickle relish
- Salad dressing

Brown ground beef in skillet; drain fat. Cool meat. Mix meat, eggs, celery and pickle relish with enough salad dressing to moisten. Spread between slices of bread or rolls.

Mrs. Glenn Kaufmann, Orrville, Ohio

POCKET BURGERS

- 1 pound ground beef
- 1/2 cup chopped onion
- 1 teaspoon salt
- 1/4 teaspoon pepper
- 1 cup sauerkraut, drained
- 1 cup shredded cheddar cheese
- 6 Hamburger buns

Brown beef and onion; add salt, pepper and sauerkraut. Heat slowly 10 minutes. Cut buns in half; scoop out a pocket in bottom and top of buns. Fill tops with shredded cheese; place under broiler to melt cheese. Fill bottom half with hot meat mixture; cover with cheese-filled top. Serve immediately.

Mrs. Betty Volkman, Hereford, Texas

CONEY ISLAND SAUCE

- 2 pounds ground beef
- 1/2 cup chopped celery
- 1/2 cup chopped onion
- 1/4 cup chopped green pepper
- 1-1/2 teaspoons salt
- 1/2 tablespoon prepared mustard
- 1-1/2 teaspoons vinegar
- 3/4 teaspoon sugar
- 1-1/2 teaspoons chili powder
- 2 cups catsup

Brown meat and vegetables; drain fat. Add remaining ingredients; simmer 1 hour. Serve over hot dogs in bun.

Kendra Ford, Waldo, Wisconsin

HAMBURGER STUFFED FRENCH BREAD

- 1 French bread
- 1 pound ground beef
- 1 green pepper, diced
- 1/2 cup diced celery
- 1 teaspoon salt
- 1/4 teaspoon pepper
- 1 tablespoon Worcestershire sauce
- 1 can condensed cheese soup, undiluted
- 6 slices American cheese

Brown beef, green pepper, celery (chopped onion, if desired) salt, pepper and Worcestershire sauce. Stir in cheese soup; simmer about 5 minutes. Cut off top of French bread; hollow out soft bread. Use bread crumbs in meat mixture, or reserve for future use. Spoon hot meat mixture into bread shell. Cut cheese to fit over top of meat. Cover with top of bread. Place on cookie sheet; bake at 350° about 10 minutes or until sandwich is warm.

Mrs. Garry Batt, Hoisington, Kansas

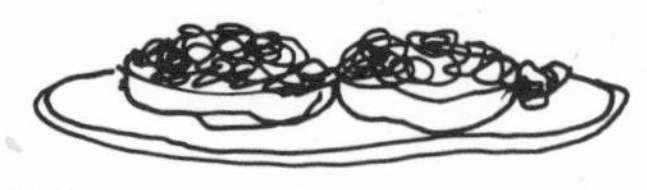

QUICK CHILI BURGERS

1 pound ground beef
1 can chili beef soup
1/2 cup water
1/2 cup shredded processed cheese
6 hamburger buns

Brown beef, blend in soup and water. Heat, stirring until mixture is hot. Cut, toast and butter buns. Spoon meat mixture on bottom bun, top with cheese; cover and serve.

Mrs. Edward Becker, Farwell, Minnesota

BARBECUED BURGERS

1 pound ground beef
1 medium-sized onion, diced
1/2 cup diced celery
1 cup sliced mushrooms
1/4 cup catsup
1 cup tomatoes
1 cup water
1 teaspoon chili powder
2 tablespoons tapioca
Hamburger buns

Brown beef, onion, celery and mushrooms in large skillet (electric works fine). Add catsup, tomatoes, water and chili powder. Salt and pepper to taste. Cover and simmer about 15 minutes. Thicken with tapioca; cook until mixture thickens. Serve over buns.

Mrs. Howard Gee, Bird Island, Minnesota

GROUND BEEF PUPS

2 pounds ground beef
1 cup blue cheese cracker crumbs OR crushed taco chips
2 tablespoons minced onion
1 cup milk
1 teaspoon salt
1/4 teaspoon pepper
1/2 teaspoon celery salt
8 ounces Monterey Jack cheese
10 slices bacon
10 hot dog buns

Combine beef with cracker crumbs, onion, milk, and seasonings. Cut the cheese into 10 equal strips about 3/8-in. thick. Divide meat mixture into 10 equal portions. Shape meat around cheese strips to form a frankfurter shape. Wrap each beef pup in slice of bacon, securing ends with wooden toothpicks. Grill 5-in. from heat, turning until bacon is crisp and pups are done. Serve in toasted, buttered buns.

Joan Aten, Las Vegas, Nevada

BARBECUED BEEF OR SLOPPY JOE SANDWICHES

- 1-1/2 pounds ground beef
- 1 cup chopped onions
- 1 cup chopped celery
- 1 green pepper, chopped (optional)
- 8 ounces tomato sauce
- 1/4 cup catsup
- 2 tablespoons brown sugar, packed
- 2 tablespoons vinegar
- 2 tablespoons barbecue sauce
- 1-2 tablespoons Worcestershire sauce
- 1 tablespoon prepared mustard
- 2 teaspoons salt
- Pepper to taste
- Hamburger buns

Brown beef and onion; drain fat. Add remaining ingredients except buns. Cover pan; simmer 1 to 2 hours to blend flavors. Serve mixture over buns.

Mrs. Janet Petersen, Utica, South Dakota

BAR-B-Q SANDWICHES

- 3 pounds beef roast
- 3 pounds ground beef
- 1 medium-sized onion, chopped
- 1-1/2 cups catsup
- 4 tablespoons brown sugar
- 2 can chicken gumbo soup, undiluted
- Salt and pepper to taste

Boil or simmer beef roast until very tender. Shred into small pieces. Brown ground beef and onion. Combine ground beef, beef roast and remaining ingredients. Simmer for 1 hour. Serve over buns.

Mrs. Esther Hershberger, Goshen, Indiana

BEEF CHEESE TURNOVERS

- Pastry dough for 2 crust pie
- 1/2 teaspoon Italian seasoning
- 1/8 teaspoon garlic powder

Filling:

- 3/4 pound ground beef
- 1 tablespoon instant onion
- 1/2 teaspoon salt
- 1 cup crumbled blue cheese
- 1-1/2 cups shredded Swiss cheese
- 3 eggs, beaten

(Continued on next page)

Prepare pastry using the seasonings if desired. Set aside. **Filling:** Brown beef with onion and salt; drain fat. Stir in cheeses then eggs; set aside. Divide pastry in half. Roll each half to rectangle 1/8-in. thick. Cut into 6-in. squares. Place about 1/4 cup filling in center of each square. Moisten edges of pastry; fold diagonally into triangle. Seal edges by pressing with tines of fork. Prick top for steam to escape while baking. Place on ungreased cookie sheet; bake at 425° 15 minutes or until lightly browned.

Mrs. Glenn Kaufmann, Orrville, Ohio

RUNZA SANDWICHES

Filling:

1 large head cabbage, shredded
2 pounds ground beef
2 large onions
Salt and pepper to taste

Dough:

2 packages active dry yeast
2 cups warm milk OR water
1/2 cup sugar
1/2 cup shortening
1 teaspoon salt
2 eggs, beaten
7-8 cups flour

Filling: Brown beef and onions in large skillet. Add shredded cabbage, salt and pepper; mix. Bring mixture to simmering point. Cover and simmer 15 minutes until cabbage is tender; stir occasionally. Cool. **Dough**: Soften yeast in warm liquid; add remaining dough ingredients, beating until smooth and satiny. Cover and let rise in warm place until doubled. Punch down, cover and let rise again. Turn out onto floured board, divide in half. Roll into rectangle about 3/8-in. thick. Cut into 5-6-in. squares. Place portion of cooled meat mixture in center of dough square. Bring corners up to center; pinching to seal seams. Place seam side down on greased cookie sheet. Let rise until doubled. Bake at 350° about 20 minutes. **Note:** If making these sandwiches to freeze, bake for only 12-15 minutes; cool completely. Wrap and freeze. To serve, remove from freezer and bake for 20 minutes. Sandwiches can be eaten in the hand, or good with melted cheese over top.

Mrs. Judith Voelker, Brownsdale, Minnesota

A DOUBLE DIP: *Save time and mess by using an ice cream scoop for shaping meat balls or hamburger patties. Just scoop and press flat with egg turner.* *Mrs. Pam Gansluckner, Maiden Rock, Wisconsin*

INDIVIDUAL MEAT PIES

Filling:

1 pound ground beef
1 onion, minced
1 clove garlic, crushed
1/2 teaspoon ground coriander
1/4 teaspoon ginger
2 cups stewed tomatoes
1/4 cup catsup
1 tablespoon brown sugar
2 tablespoons parsley
1/2 teaspoon salt
1/8 teaspoon pepper

Egg Pastry:

2-3/4 cups flour
1/2 teaspoon salt
2/3 cup shortening
2 egg yolks
1/2 cup cold water

Brown beef, onion and garlic. Add remaining filling ingredients, cook until thickened; cool. **Egg Pastry:** Add salt to flour, cut in shortening until mixture resembles crumbs. Beat egg yolks, add water; mix well. Stir into flour mixture until dough forms. Roll out, cut into 6-in. circles. Place 1/3 cup filling on each circle. Moisten edges, fold over and seal with tines of fork. Cut steam vents in top. Bake at 375° 25 to 35 minutes until golden brown. Yield: 8 pies.

Vivian Biggs, Valparaiso, Indiana

BEEF PEEK-A-BOOS

1-1/2 pounds ground beef
1/2 cup cream of celery soup, undiluted
1/4 cup finely chopped onion
1/4 cup water
3/4 cup soft bread crumbs
1 teaspoon salt
1/8 teaspoon pepper
1/2 teaspoon sage

Pastry:

2 cups flour
1 tablespoon baking powder
3/4 teaspoon salt
4-6 tablespoons lard
1/3 to 1/2 cup milk

Combine beef with remaining ingredients. Mix well. Shape into 12 mounds; place on ungreased baking pan. **Pastry:** Mix as for pie dough by combining dry ingredients. Cut in lard until crumbs form. Stir in enough milk to make soft dough. Turn onto floured board; knead 1/2 minute. Roll dough to 12- x 16-in. rectangle; cut into 12 4- x 4-in. squares. Make 2 cuts 1-1/2-in. long through center of square to form an X. Place square of pastry over each mound of meat. Bake at 400° 30 minutes. Make gravy by heating remaining celery soup with 1/3 to 1/2 cup milk. Serve over Beef Peek-a-boos.

Mrs. Edgar Ahnemann, Alden, Minnesota

Meatballs

SWEDISH MEATBALLS

2 tablespoons butter
1 medium onion, minced
1 egg, beaten
2 slices fresh bread, crumbled
1/2 cup milk
1-1/4 teaspoons salt
2 teaspoons sugar
1/2 teaspoon ground allspice
1/4 teaspoon nutmeg
1 pound ground beef
2 tablespoons butter

Gravy:
3 tablespoons flour
1 teaspoon sugar
Salt and pepper to taste
1 cup water
3/4 cup light cream OR evaporated milk

Saute onions in butter until glossy. In bowl, beat egg; add bread and milk. Let stand 5 minutes. Add salt, pepper, sugar, spices and meat. Add onion; mix well. Shape meat mixture into balls, the size you desire. Brown in butter. Place meatballs in ovenproof casserole dish. Add flour to butter in skillet meat was browned in. Stir to blend. Add sugar, salt and pepper. Slowly stir in water, stirring until mixture is smooth and beginning to thicken. Stir in cream, blending until sauce is bubbly and thickened. Pour over meatballs, cover and bake at 325° 1 hour. *Hazel Kout, Walker, Iowa*

MEATBALLS SUPREME

2 eggs
1 cup applesauce
1 cup oatmeal
2 teaspoons salt
1/4 teaspoon pepper
2 pounds ground beef
1/2 cup finely chopped onion

Sauce:
1/4 cup finely chopped celery
1/4 cup finely chopped carrot
1/4 cup finely chopped onion
2 tablespoons chopped green pepper
2 tablespoons sugar
2 tablespoons flour
1/2 teaspoon salt
2 cups tomato juice

Beat eggs in large mixing bowl. Add applesauce, oatmeal, salt and pepper; stir. Add meat and onions; mix well. Chill several hours. Shape into balls size of walnut. Arrange meat balls in single layer in large baking dish. **Sauce:** Combine ingredients; pour over meatballs. Bake, uncovered at 325° 40 to 50 minutes. *Mrs. Fred Kraemer, Glencoe, Minnesota*

SAVORY MEATBALLS WITH BISCUITS

Meatballs:

1 pound ground beef
1/4 pound bulk pork sausage
1/2 cup dried bread crumbs
1/3 cup evaporated milk
2 tablespoons chopped onion
1/2 teaspoon chili powder
1/8 teaspoon pepper

Sauce:

1 can cream of mushroom soup
1 can cream of celery soup
1 cup evaporated milk
1/2 cup water

Chili Cheese Biscuits:

1-1/3 cups flour
3 teaspoons baking powder
1/2 teaspoon chili powder
1/4 teaspoon salt
1/3 cup shortening
1 egg, unbeaten
1/3 cup milk
1-1/2 cups shredded cheddar cheese
1 tablespoon parsley

Combine meatball ingredients, shape into small balls; brown and cook about 10 minutes. Place meatballs in 10- x 8-in. baking dish. Combine sauce ingredients, heat and pour over meatballs. **Biscuits:** Sift flour, baking powder, chili powder and salt. Cut in shortening as for pie dough. Combine egg and milk; add to dry ingredients, stirring only until dough is moistened. Knead 10 strokes, roll out to 12-in. square; sprinkle with cheddar cheese and parsley. Roll jelly roll fashion; cut into 12 slices. Arrange on top of meatballs; bake at 400° 20 to 25 minutes.

Mrs. A.L. Vogel, Sutherland, Iowa

2,000 BAKED MEATBALLS

Meatballs:

100 pounds ground beef
40 eggs
55 pounds soft bread crumbs
25 cups milk
9 pounds onions, chopped
20 tablespoons sugar
16 tablespoons plus 2 teaspoons salt
2-1/2 cups Worcestershire sauce

Sauce:

3 pounds 12 ounces butter
1 pound 14 ounces flour
10 quarts milk
20 tablespoons Worcestershire sauce
10 tablespoons salt
Paprika

Combine meatball ingredients; mix well. Shape into balls and place on large baking sheets. Bake at 325° for 45 minutes. Pour off drippings. **Sauce**: Melt butter, add flour to make a smooth paste. Add milk gradually, stirring constantly until mixture thickens. Add Worcestershire sauce and salt. Pour sauce over meatballs and sprinkle with paprika. Return to oven and bake 45 to 50 minutes or until meatballs are lightly browned. *National Meat Board*

DEVILISHLY DELICIOUS MEATBALLS

1/4 pound Roquefort cheese, crumbled
1/4 cup mayonnaise
2 tablespoons Worcestershire sauce
1 teaspoon prepared mustard
1 egg, slightly beaten
1/2 cup milk
2 cups cornflakes, crushed
1-1/1 teaspoons salt
1/8 teaspoon pepper
1 pound ground beef
1 can golden mushroom soup
1/4 cup water

Blend cheese, mayonnaise, Worcestershire sauce and mustard. Combine egg, milk, cornflakes, seasoning and beef; mix well. Add cheese; mix well. Shape into balls; broil until browned. Or saute in butter until browned. Combine soup and water; heat until mixture simmers. Pour over meatballs, serve hot. *Helen M. Haaland, Woodbury, Connecticut*

SURPRISE MEATBALLS

1/2 pound ground beef
2/3 cup soft bread crumbs
1 egg, beaten
2 tablespoons finely chopped onion
1/2 teaspoon Worcestershire sauce
1/4 teaspoon salt
Pimiento stuffed green olives
Cocktail onions
Pineapple tidbits
Small whole mushrooms
Cheese cubes 1/2-in. square

Sauce:
1 cup catsup
4 teaspoons brown sugar
4 teaspoons prepared mustard
6 drops bottled hot pepper sauce

Combine beef, crumbs, egg, onion, Worcestershire sauce and salt. Mix well. Shape spoonful of meat around any of the listed olives, onions, pineapple, mushrooms or cheese. Bake at 425° about 10 minutes. Heat sauce ingredients until mixture simmers. Pour over meatballs or serve as a dip sauce.
Mrs. Alicia Jackson, Uniontown, Kansas

PIZZA MEATBALLS

1 pound ground beef
1 egg, slightly beaten
1/4 cup chopped onion
1/2 teaspoon salt
1/4 teaspoon black pepper
12 1/2-in. cubes mozarella cheese
2 tablespoons vegetable oil
3/4 cup catsup
4 ounces canned mushroom pieces
1/2 teaspoon Italian seasoning
1 clove garlic, crushed

Lightly mix beef, egg, onion, salt and pepper. Form 12 meatballs around the cheese chunks. Brown meatballs lightly on all sides in hot oil. Drain oil from skillet. Add remaining ingredients into frypan including mushroom juice. Blend gently; add meatballs. Cover and simmer about 15 minutes. Serves 4.

Mrs. Darrell DeBoer, Corsica, South Dakota

VIKING MEATBALLS

1-1/2 pounds ground beef
3/4 cup Zweibach OR bread crumbs
1 cup dairy sour cream
1/4 cup minced onion
1/2 cup butter
1 teaspoon salt
1/8 teaspoon pepper
1/2 teaspoon nutmeg
2 egg yolks
1 cup beef bouillon
1/2 cup Burgundy cooking wine

Combine crumbs with sour cream; add beef, mix well. Saute onion lightly in butter. Add to meat mixture with seasonings and egg yolks; mix well. Shape into small balls; brown in butter. Cover with bouillon and wine; cook at simmer for 1 hour.

Helen Haaland, Woodbury, Connecticut

SALISBURY MEATBALLS

2 pounds ground beef
1-1/2 cups cracker crumbs
2 eggs
1/2 cup catsup
2 tablespoons diced onion
2 teaspoons parsley
1 teaspoon Worcestershire sauce
1-1/2 teaspoons salt
1/2 teaspoon pepper
1/2 teaspoon marjoram
1/2 teaspoon nutmeg

Sauce:
1 can cream of mushroom soup
8-ounce can mushrooms
1/4 teaspoon garlic salt
1 cup barbecue sauce

Combine meat ingredients until well blended. Shape into balls and
browned. Combine sauce ingredients, pour over meatballs; bal
about 45 minutes. Good served over rice or noodles.

Mrs. Donald Rupert, New Waterford, Ohio

SAVORY COCKTAIL MEATBALLS

2 pounds ground beef
4 slices bread, crumbled
Milk to soften crumbs
1/2 cup grated Parmesan cheese
1/2 cup snipped parsley
1/2 tablespoon sweet basil
2 cloves garlic, minced
3 teaspoons salt
1/2 teaspoon black pepper
3 eggs

Sauce:
3/4 cup brown sugar
12 ounces chili sauce
1/2 cup vinegar
1/2 cup pineapple juice
1/2 cup oil
2 teaspoons prepared mustard
2 teaspoons Worcestershire sauce

In large bowl combine softened bread crumbs with enough milk to moisten. Add remaining meatball ingredients, blending well. Shape meat mixture into 1-in. balls, roll in flour then brown in hot oil. Combine the sauce ingredients, simmering to blend flavors. Place meatballs in large flat casserole, pour sauce over meat and bake at 350° 30 to 40 minutes.

Mrs. Muriel Sawyers, Willits, California

COCKTAIL MEATBALLS

1 pound ground beef
1/2 cup dry bread crumbs
1/3 cup minced onion
1/4 cup milk
1 egg
1 tablespoon snipped parsley
1 teaspoon salt
1/8 teaspoon pepper
1/2 teaspoon Worcestershire sauce
12-ounce bottle chili sauce
10-ounce jar grape jelly

Combine first 9 ingredients; mix well. Shape into small meatballs; brown in small amount of oil. Heat the chili sauce and grape jelly together. Drain fat from skillet meatballs were browned in. Return meat to skillet, pour chili mixture over meat; cover and simmer about 30 minutes. Serve in chafing dish or fondue pot.

Mrs. Connie Braet, Eldridge, Iowa

AMBURGER STROGANOFF

1-1/2 pounds ground beef
2 tablespoons shortening
1 cup sliced onions
1 package Kraft Sour Cream Sauce mix
1/2 cup salad dressing
1 beef bouillon cube
1-1/3 cups boiling water
1/4 pound fresh mushrooms OR 4 ounces canned
1/4 teaspoon pepper
Rice OR noodles

Shape beef into 1-in. balls. Brown in shortening on all sides. Add onions and cook until onions are glossy. Combine Kraft sauce mix with salad dressing; stir into meat mixture. Dissolve bouillon cube in boiling water; add to meat. Add mushrooms and pepper; cover and simmer 20 minutes. Serve over rice or noodles. *Mrs. Alice Walker, Blue Mound, Kansas*

FANCY FRENCH MEATBALLS

2 pounds ground beef
1 cup fine bread crumbs
2 garlic cloves, minced
2 medium-sized onions, chopped
1 tablespoon chopped parsley
2-1/2 teaspoons salt
1/2 teaspoon pepper
5 tablespoons flour, divided
2 tablespoons butter
1 cup dry red wine
10-1/2 ounces condensed beef broth
1 beef bouillon cube
1/2 pound mushrooms, whole or sliced

Combine meat, bread crumbs, garlic, onion, parsley, salt and pepper; mix well. Form into 12 meatballs; roll in 2 tablespoons flour. Refrigerate. Melt butter in large fry pan, brown meatballs on all sides. Sprinkle remaining flour over meatballs. Add wine, beef broth, bouillon cube; simmer 10 minutes. Add mushrooms; simmer 10 minutes more, or until meatballs are done to your liking. Serves 6. *Sue Ward, Milwaukee, Wisconsin*

MEATBALLS STROGANOFF

1 pound ground beef
1 teaspoon salt
1/4 teaspoon pepper
1/4 cup catsup
1 tablespoon Worcestershire sauce
1/4 cup minced onion
1/2 cup bread crumbs
1/2 cup evaporated milk

Sauce:

1 cup evaporated milk
10-3/4-ounce can cream of mushroom soup
1 tablespoon cider vinegar
1-1/2 teaspoons Worcestershire sauce

Combine meat ingredients; mix well. Shape into 16 meatballs, roll in flour and brown in oil on all sides. Drain fat; arrange meatballs in 1-1/2-quart casserole. Combine sauce ingredients pour over meatballs. Bake at 350° 20 to 30 minutes until bubbly. *Mrs. Gail Lambert, Winamac, Illinois*

WAIKIKI MEATBALLS

1-1/2 pounds ground beef
2/3 cup soda cracker crumbs
1 small onion, diced
1 egg
1 teaspoon salt
1/4 teaspoon ginger
1/4 cup milk
1 tablespoon shortening
2 tablespoons cornstarch
1/2 cup brown sugar
13-1/2-ounce can pineapple tidbits, reserve juice
1/3 cup vinegar
1 tablespoon soy sauce
1/3 cup chopped green pepper

Mix beef, crumbs, onion, egg, salt, ginger and milk. Shape into 1-in. balls. Brown meatballs in shortening. Remove from pan; drain fat. Combine cornstarch and brown sugar, stir in reserved pineapple juice, vinegar and soy sauce. Mix until smooth. Pour into frypan; cook until thickened. Boil 1 minute. Add green pepper, pineapple tidbits and meatballs, heat thoroughly.
Mrs. Sherman Schnell, Kiel, Wisconsin

TACO MEATBALLS

1 pound ground beef
1 cup each finely chopped onions green pepper and celery
2 cups cooked rice
2 eggs, beaten
2 teaspoons garlic salt
8-ounce can taco sauce
11-ounce can condensed cheddar cheese soup

Combine meat, onions, green pepper, celery, rice, eggs and garlic salt. Mix well, form into 12 meatballs. Place in lightly greased 2-1/2-quart casserole. Bake at 350° for 30 minutes. Blend and heat taco sauce and soup. Pour over meatballs; cover and continue baking 30 minutes longer. Yield: 6 servings.
Rice Council of America

MEATBALLS PIZZA STYLE

- 1 pound ground beef
- 1 cup dried bread crumbs
- 1/2 cup milk
- 2 tablespoons instant minced onion
- 1 teaspoon garlic salt
- 1/4 teaspoon oregano
- 1/8 teaspoon pepper
- 4 ounces mozzarella cheese, cut into bite size cubes
- 3 tablespoons flour
- 2 teaspoons oil
- 2 10-1/2-ounce cans pizza sauce
- 4 cups cooked rice

Combine ground beef, crumbs, milk, onion, salt, oregano and pepper; mix well. Divide meat mixture into 12 equal portions. Shape into balls around a cube of cheese. Roll each ball in flour. Brown meatballs in oil; drain fat. Add pizza sauce, bring to boil. Reduce heat to low; simmer gently 10 to 15 minutes. Serve over rice. Serves 6.

Mrs. Debbie Harker, Waldron, Indiana

TASTY MEAT LOAF LEFTOVERS: *Slice cold meat loaf, dip it in your favorite batter then roll in bread crumbs or crushed cornflakes. Saute until crisp and warmed through.* *Mrs. Doris Riddle, Worden, Montana*

CHIPS, NOT CRUMBS: *Use crushed potato chips instead of bread crumbs for meat loaf filler. The flavor will make an excellent addition.*

Mrs. Clarence Huss, Hartington, Nebraska

MEAT LOAF'S IN THE BAG: *Place ingredients in large plastic bag, close tightly with a wire twist. Squeeze and knead bag until blended. Slide meat mixture out of bag into roasting pan. Shape and bake.*

Mrs. Hilda C. Pafe, Elgin, Nebraska

RICE IS NICE: *Add 1 cup cooked rice to your meat loaf. Adds moisture, slices firmly and tastes delicious.*

Mrs. Amos Hoover, Denver, Pennsylvania

Meat Loaf

ZESTY MEAT LOAF

2 pounds ground beef
2 eggs
3/4 cup milk
1-1/2 cups soft bread crumbs
2 medium-sized carrots, grated
1/3 cup minced onion
2 teaspoons salt
1/8 teaspoon lemon pepper OR pepper

Sauce:
1/4 cup catsup
3 tablespoons brown sugar
2 tablespoons prepared mustard

Mix meat loaf ingredients well. Shape into loaf and place in 13- x 9-in. pan, or pack into 9- x 5-in. bread pan. Mix sauce ingredients together. Spread over meat. Bake at 300° 1-1/2 hours.

Latona Mae Erickson, Wheaton, Minnesota

APRICOT MEAT LOAF

1-1/2 pounds ground beef
1/2 pound ground pork
8 slices bacon, minced
1-1/2 cups soft bread crumbs
1/2 cup minced onion
2 tablespoons fresh parsley, minced OR 1 teaspoon dried parsley flakes
1/4 cup evaporated milk
1 tablespoon Worcestershire sauce
1/4 teaspoon lemon rind
1/4 teaspoon poultry seasoning
1/4 teaspoon paprika
1/4 teaspoon marjoram
1 teaspoon salt
1/4 teaspoon pepper
1 egg, slightly beaten
1/4 to 1/2 cup apricot syrup
1-pound can apricot halves
3 teaspoons brown sugar

Mix all ingredients except apricots and brown sugar. Pack into 9- x 5- x 3-in. loaf pan. Press drained apricot halves into top of meat loaf. Bake at 350° 1 hour. Drain off fat and liquid. Sprinkle top with brown sugar; bake 30 minutes more.

Mrs. Wayne Meade, Parnell, Iowa

MYSTERY MINI LOAVES

1-1/2 cups soft bread crumbs
1/2 cup beef stock, water OR milk
1 package dry onion soup mix
3 eggs, beaten
3 pounds ground beef

Sauce:

12-ounce bottle chili sauce
1-1/3 cups water
1/2 cup brown sugar
16 ounces sauerkraut, drained
16 ounces whole cranberry sauce

Soak crumbs in beef stock. Add beaten eggs and onion soup mix; stir. Add ground beef; mix well. Shape into individual loaves, size desired. Place in greased 13- x 9-in. baking pan. **Sauce:** Combine ingredients; simmer 5 minutes. Pour over meat loaves and bake at 350° until meat is done. Timing will vary depending upon size of loaves. **Note:** 10 small loaves bake about 1 hour and 10 minutes. *Catherine Schmidt, Angola, Indiana*

GARDEN PRIZE MEAT LOAF

3 large potatoes, peeled
2 large onions, peeled
1 large green pepper
1 apple, peeled and cored
1 carrot, peeled
1-3/4 pounds ground beef
1/4 pound sausage
1/4 cup soda cracker crumbs
1/4 cup cream or evaporated milk
2 teaspoons salt
1/4 teaspoon pepper
2 eggs, slightly beaten
8 ounces tomato sauce

Coarsely chop potatoes, onions, green pepper, apple and carrot. Mix thoroughly with remaining ingredients, except tomato sauce. Shape into 9- x 5- x 3-in. loaf pan or 2-quart casserole dish. Pour tomato sauce over top. Bake at 350° 1-1/2 hours. Let stand about 10 minutes before turning out onto serving dish. *Mrs. Orpha Culver, Hanna City, Illinois*

WORLD'S BEST MEAT LOAF

1 egg
1 teaspoon salt
1/4 teaspoon pepper
1/2 teaspoon basil
1 teaspoon monosodium glutamate
1/4 cup catsup
2 teaspoons prepared mustard
2 beef bouillon cubes
1 cup boiling water
1-1/2 cups bread crumbs
1/2 cup chopped celery
1/2 cup chopped onion
1 cup shredded cheddar cheese
2 pounds ground beef

Beat egg, add salt, pepper, spices, catsup and mustard. Dissolve bouillon cubes in boiling water; add to egg mixture; mix well. Add bread crumbs, celery, onion and cheese. Add ground beef; mix well. Shape into loaf; bake at 375° 1 hour. *Cathy Smith, Liberal, Kansas*

MEAT LOAF WITH DILL SAUCE

1-1/2 pounds ground beef
1/4 cup chopped onion
1/2 cup soft bread crumbs
1/2 cup dill pickle juice
1 egg
1-1/2 teaspoons salt
1/4 teaspoon pepper

Sauce:
1/2 cup chopped dill pickle
1/4 cup water
2 tablespoons sugar
1/2 cup catsup
1 teaspoon Worcestershire sauce

Combine meat loaf ingredients, mix well. Shape into loaf and place in baking pan. Combine sauce ingredients; mix well. Pour about half the sauce carefully over top of meat loaf. Reserve remaining sauce, spooning it over meat loaf during baking period. Bake at 350° 1 hour and 15 minutes.

Jean Piest, Columbia, Missouri

NUTRITIOUS MEAT LOAF

1-1/2 pounds ground beef
3/4 cup quick cooking oatmeal
3 teaspoons brewer's yeast
3 tablespoons wheat germ
1 egg, beaten
1/4 cup chopped onion
1-1/2 teaspoons sea salt
1-1/2 cups V-8 vegetable juice OR tomato juice

Mix all ingredients well. Pack into 8- x 4- x 2-in. pan. Bake at 350° 1 hour and 15 minutes. Cool 5 minutes before slicing.

Mrs. Rod Aden, Santa Rosa, California

FAVORITE MEAT LOAF

2 pounds ground beef
1/4 cup chopped onion
2 tablespoons chopped celery OR green pepper
2 teaspoons salt
1/2 teaspoon poultry seasoning
1/4 teaspoon pepper
1/4 teaspoon dry mustard
1 tablespoon Worcestershire sauce
4 slices soft bread, cut into cubes
1/2 cup milk
2 eggs, slightly beaten

Combine ingredients; mixing well to blend. Shape into loaf in large shallow baking pan. Bake at 350° 1-1/2 hours.

Mrs. Fred Aberle, Sabetha, Kansas

PIZZA MEAT LOAF

10-3/4-ounce can tomato soup
1/4 cup water
1-1/2 teaspoons Italian seasoning
1/4 teaspoon garlic salt
2 pounds ground beef
1 cup bread crumbs, dry
1/4 cup chopped onion
2 tablespoons chopped parsley
1 egg, beaten
1 teaspoons salt
1/8 teaspoon pepper
2 ounces shredded cheese (1/2 cup)

Mix soup, water, Italian seasoning and garlic salt. Set aside. Mix beef with remaining ingredients, except cheese. Pour in 1/2 of soup mixture; blend well. Shape into loaf and place in large shallow baking dish or loaf bread pan. Bake at 350° 1 hour. Pour remaining soup over top, sprinkle with cheese; return to oven until cheese melts. *Mrs. Dale E. Kraft, Corwith, Iowa*

CHEESE MEAT LOAF

1-1/2 pounds ground beef
2 teaspoons salt
1-1/2 cups dry bread crumbs
2 eggs, beaten
2/3 cup diced American cheese
2 tablespoons chopped green pepper
1/2 cup chopped onion
Dash thyme
Small bay leaf, crushed
1-1/4 cups tomato sauce OR tomato soup (undiluted)

Combine ingredients; mix well. Shape into 1 or 2 loaves. Place in shallow baking pan. Bake at 350° 1 hour for large loaf, about 35 minutes for small loaves. *Cora G. Reese, Macy, Indiana*

MOCK HAM LOAF

1 pound ground beef
1/2 pound bologna OR frankfurters, ground
1 egg, beaten
1 teaspoon salt
1/4 teaspoon pepper
1 cup soda cracker crumbs

Glaze:
3/4 cup brown sugar
1/2 cup water
1 tablespoon vinegar
1/2 teaspoon dry mustard

Bring glaze ingredients to boil. Cool slightly. Mix meat loaf ingredients together; add 1/2 syrup mixture, blend well. Place in 9- x 5- x 3-in. loaf pan. Pour remaining syrup over top; bake at 350° 1 hour.

Mrs. Alvin Stoftzfus, Oxford, Pennsylvania

MEAT LOAF SOUFFLE

1-1/2 pounds ground beef
1 egg
1/2 cup bread crumbs
1/2 cup chopped onion
1/2 cup milk
1-1/2 teaspoons salt
1/8 teaspoon pepper
4 ounces sliced or shredded cheddar cheese

Topping:
1 cup sour cream
3/4 cup flour
3 eggs, separated
1/2 teaspoon salt
Dash pepper

Combine ground beef, egg, crumbs, onion, milk, salt and pepper; mix well. Pat into 9-in. square baking dish; bake at 350° 25 minutes. Drain off fat. Top with cheese. **Topping:** Beat egg white stiff but not dry. Combine sour cream, flour, egg yolks, salt and pepper. Fold in egg whites. Carefully spread over cheese. Return to oven and bake 30 to 40 minutes more until golden brown. Cool 5 minutes before serving.

Mrs. Karen Larson, Rothsay, Minnesota

COMBINATION MEAT LOAVES

2-1/2 pounds ground ham
2 pounds ground pork
1 pound ground beef
3 eggs, beaten
3 cups graham cracker crumbs
2 cups milk

Sauce:
2 cans tomato soup, undiluted
3/4 cup vinegar
2 cups brown sugar
2 teaspoons dry mustard

Combine meats, eggs, crumbs and milk; mix well. Shape into small individual loaves (about 25). Place in large baking dish leaving space between each loaf. **Sauce:** Combine ingredients; pour over loaves and bake at 350° 1 hour. Baste loaves several times during baking. **Note:** Recipe may be used for appetizers. Shape meat mixture into 1-in. balls. Place in large baking dish; pour sauce over balls and bake about 35 minutes, or until meatballs are done. Serves 10.

Joan Aten, Las Vegas, Nevada

BACON LINER: *Line a loaf pan with strips of bacon, pack in meat mixture and bake. Bacon adds flavor, meat loaf looks pretty and never gets too brown on bottom.*

Mrs. Curtis Sykora, Windom, Minnesota

Mexican Dishes

ENCHILADAS

1 dozen frozen corn tortillas, thawed
1-1/2 cups shredded sharp cheddar cheese

Gravy:
1/2 cup salad oil
2/3 cup flour
1/4 cup chili powder
2 teaspoons salt
1 quart cold water
1 can cream of tomato soup

Filling:
1-1/2 pounds ground beef
2 large onions, chopped
1 small can chopped olives
1-1/2 teaspoons salt
8 ounces tomato sauce

Gravy: Stir flour into salad oil add chili powder, salt, water and soup. Heat until boiling, stirring occasionally; set aside. Meanwhile brown beef and onion; add olives, salt and tomato sauce; simmer 15 minutes. Dip each tortilla in gravy, allow to drip then lay flat on a plate. Place large spoonful of meat mixture on tortilla, fold one side over the other, fasten with toothpicks. Place in 13- x 9-in. baking dish. Repeat with remaining tortillas. Spoon any leftover meat over tortillas, pour gravy over all and sprinkle with shredded cheese. Bake at 350° about 40 minutes until sauce is hot and bubbly.

Mrs. Muriel Sawyers, Willits, California

MEXICAN DINNER

1 pound ground beef
1 small onion, chopped
1/4 cup diced celery
15 ounces tomato sauce
1/2 teaspoon salt
1 teaspoon chili powder
Dash pepper
Dash oregano

Topping:
1/2 cup cornmeal
1/2 cup flour
2 tablespoons sugar
2 teaspoons baking powder
1/4 teaspoon salt
1 small egg
1/2 cup milk
2 tablespoons shortening, softened

Brown beef and onion. Add celery, sauce and seasonings; heat through. Pour into 8-in. square pan. Combine corn meal, flour, sugar, baking powder and salt. Add egg, milk and shortening. Beat until smooth. Spread over hamburger mixture. Bake at 425° 20-25 minutes until golden.

Mrs. Cynthia Kammerer, Winona, Minnesota

MEXICAN LASAGNA

4 cups chopped tomatoes (fresh or drained canned)
2-1/2 to 3 cups spaghetti sauce with mushrooms
1/2 cup pitted ripe olives, sliced
2 pounds ground beef
2 cups chopped onion
2 teaspoons salt
3/4 teaspoon pepper
2 cups chopped celery
1 cup chopped green pepper
2 cups shredded sharp cheddar cheese
2 cups creamed cottage cheese
2 eggs, slightly beaten
16 taco shells, broken
4 taco shells, quartered
1 cup shredded sharp cheddar cheese

In large saucepan, combine the tomatoes, spaghetti sauce and olives; simmer gently. In skillet, brown beef and onion, season with salt and pepper. Add beef mixture, celery and green pepper to tomato sauce. Simmer covered, 20 minutes, stirring occasionally. Combine cheeses and egg. Spread 1/3 of meat mixture in 14- x 10-in. baking pan. Top with 1/2 of cheese mixture. Then layer 1/2 broken taco shells on cheese. Repeat layers ending with meat mixture. Top with 4 quartered taco shells. Sprinkle 1 cup shredded cheese over top. Bake at 350° 30 minutes. Allow to stand 5 minutes before serving.

Mrs. Glenn Spray, Mt. Vernon, Ohio

MEXICANA BEEF DISH

2 pounds ground beef
1 green pepper, chopped
1 clove garlic, minced
2 teaspoons onion salt OR 1 onion, chopped
1/2 teaspoon black pepper
1 tablespoon brown sugar
1 tablespoon chili powder
1 package taco seasoning mix
15 ounces tomato sauce
10-ounce can enchilada sauce
1-1/2 cups water
1 tablespoon cornmeal
1 can chili with beans
1 cup shredded sharp cheddar cheese
3 cups corn chips
1 cup sour cream

In large skillet or Dutch oven brown meat, green pepper, garlic and onion. Drain off fat. Add seasonings, sauces and water; simmer about 15 minutes. Thicken with cornmeal. Add chili with beans; stir in 1/2 cup cheese and 2 cups corn chips. Pour into casserole dish; bake at 350° 25 minutes until hot. Spread sour cream over top; sprinkle with remaining cheese and 1 cup crushed corn chips. Bake 5 minutes more. Serves 12.

Mrs. Carolyn Womack, Ashford, Alabama

BAKED ENCHILADAS

- 1 pound ground beef
- 1 medium sized onion, chopped
- 1 teaspoon chili powder
- 1 teaspoon salt
- 1 can cream of chicken soup, divided
- 15 ounces tomato sauce
- 2 teaspoons chili powder
- Dash cayenne or tabasco
- 1/8 teaspoon garlic powder
- 1 dozen tortillas
- 1-1/2 cups shredded cheese (half Jack and half cheddar)

Brown beef and onion; add 1 teaspoon chili powder, salt and 1/2 can soup. Simmer about 15 minutes. Meanwhile combine tomato sauce, 2 teaspoons chili powder, cayenne and garlic powder; simmer. Add small amount of water if sauce is too thick. Fry the tortillas in skillet with small amount of hot fat, 30 seconds on each side. Drain on paper towel. Roll up a large spoonful of meat mixture in each tortilla; secure with toothpick and lay in shallow baking dish. Pour sauce over enchiladas and sprinkle with cheese. Bake at 375° about 30 minutes or until brown and bubbly.

Rhea Jean Lease, Bismarck, North Dakota

CHILI RELLENAS

- 1 pound ground beef
- Salt and pepper
- 2 small cans whole green chilies
- 2 cups shredded cheddar cheese
- 1 cup finely chopped onions
- 4 eggs
- 1/4 cup flour
- 3/4 cup milk
- 3 drops hot pepper sauce

Brown ground beef, season with salt and pepper. Remove seeds from chilies; spread 1 can of chilies over bottom of 9-in. square baking dish. Layer 1/2 of ground beef, cheese and onions over chilies. Repeat layers with remaining half of ingredients. Beat eggs, add flour, milk, dash salt and hot pepper sauce. Pour over casserole. Bake at 375° 35-40 minutes. Let stand 5 minutes; cut into squares.

Lucy Dick, Englevale, North Dakota

MEXICAN HAMBURGER STEW

- 1 to 2 pounds ground beef
- 1 medium-sized onion, chopped
- Salt and pepper
- 19-ounce can chunky vegetable soup
- 29-1/2-ounce can chili style beans in chili gravy

10-1/2-ounce can cream of tomato soup
Chili powder to taste
Corn chips

Brown beef and onion, season to taste. Add soups, beans and season with chili powder to taste. Simmer gently until flavors mingle and stew is hot. Serve in bowls garnished with corn chips.

Mrs. Judith A. Davis, Fort Dodge, Iowa

TACO SALAD

2 pounds ground beef
1 package dry taco seasoning mix
3/4 cup water
1 can Mexican chili beans, drained
1 head lettuce, coarsely shredded
1 medium onion, chopped
4 medium tomatoes, chopped
1 pound cheddar cheese, shredded
1 package corn or taco flavored chips
1 8-ounce bottle taco sauce
1 8-ounce bottle dressing, (Catalina or Thousand Island)

Brown beef, drain fat. Add taco seasoning mix, water and chili beans. Simmer about 10 minutes. Just before serving, toss salad ingredients with enough taco sauce and dressing to coat well. Serve immediately. Serves 10 to 12.

Helen Koehn, Livingston, California

MUSCATELLO

1 pound ground beef
1 pound pork sausage
3 onions, diced
1 large green pepper, diced
1 large can mushrooms
2 teaspoons chili powder (or to taste)
1 teaspoon sugar
1 can kernel corn, undrained
2 tablespoons Worcestershire sauce
2 large cans tomato paste
Salt and pepper
1-1/2-pound package macaroni
1/2 pound cheddar cheese, diced

Brown the beef, sausage, onion and green pepper. Add mushrooms, chili powder, sugar, corn, Worcestershire sauce, tomato paste, salt and pepper. Simmer gently about 15 minutes. Cook macaroni according to directions on package until nearly done—do not overcook! Combine meat mixture, macaroni and cheese. Pour into large casserole; bake at 350° 1 hour. Serves 10.

Mrs. Edwin Weber, Nauvoo, Illinois

TORTILLAS AMERICANA

3/4 cup yellow cornmeal
9.5-ounce can refrigerated buttermilk biscuits
1/3 cup melted butter
1 pound ground beef
1 tablespoon salad oil
1 cup chopped fresh tomatoes
1 cup shredded sharp cheddar cheese
1/4 cup chopped onion
1/4 cup chopped ripe olives
1 teaspoon salt
Dash tabasco
2 cups shredded lettuce

Preheat oven to 400°. Sprinkle wooden board or pastry cloth with thin layer of cornmeal. Roll 1 biscuit at a time into a 6-in. circle, turning to coat each side. Place on greased cookie sheet; brush lightly with melted butter. Bake 2 to 3 minutes until lightly browned. Turn, brush with butter; bake 2 to 3 minutes. Keep biscuits warm. Brown beef in oil; drain off fat. Stir in tomatoes, 1/2 cup cheese, onion, olives, salt and tabasco. Heat to serving temperature, stirring frequently. Top each tortilla with an equal amount of beef mixture, lettuce and a sprinkling of remaining cheese. Serves 5.

Barbara J. Rubino, Billerica, Massachusetts

CARNE DE VACA CREPES

Crepes:
3/4 cup flour
1/2 cup cornmeal
Dash salt
1-1/4 cups milk
3 eggs
1 tablespoon melted butter

Filling:
2 pounds ground beef
2 packages taco seasoning mix
2 teaspoons cornmeal
1 cup shredded mild cheddar cheese

Combine crepe ingredients; beat on medium speed of electric mixer until smooth. Fry about 1/4 cup batter in greased 6-in. skillet until crepe is browned on one side and top is shiny. Place on paper towel. Proceed until all batter is baked. Brown beef; drain fat. Stir in cornmeal and taco seasoning mix prepared according to directions on package. Place meat mixture on pancake, dividing evenly for crepes baked. Roll up and place seam side down on greased baking dish. Sprinkle with shredded cheese; bake at 400° at least 10 minutes to melt cheese and warm crepes. Serve on bed of shredded lettuce, garnished with wedges of tomatoes, olives, more cheese and your choice of taco sauce.

Mrs. Renae Doan, McKenzie, North Dakota

TACOS

- 1 head lettuce, shredded
- 4 medium-sized tomatoes, chopped
- 4 to 8 ounces cheese, shredded (your favorite kind)
- 1-1/2 pounds ground beef
- 1 cup cold water
- 1/4 cup chopped onion
- 1-1/2 cups unseasoned mashed potatoes
- 1 teaspoon garlic salt
- 2 teaspoons salt
- Dash pepper
- 1/4 cup chili sauce
- 2 teaspoons chili powder (or to taste)
- 1/2 teaspoon ground cumin
- Taco shells
- Dash taco sauce, optional

Set lettuce, tomatoes and cheese aside. Mix water and onion into ground beef. Place in skillet over low heat; cook, stirring often until meat is browned. Stir potatoes into meat mixture. Add garlic salt, salt and pepper, chili sauce, chili powder and cumin. Simmer until mixture is thick and pasty. Spoon meat mixture into taco shells. Top each with spoonful of lettuce, tomatoes then cheese. Add dash of taco sauce if desired.

Mrs. Sheryl L. Busse, St. Cloud, Minnesota

TALLERENE

- 2 pounds ground beef
- 2 onions, chopped
- 8 ounces wide egg noodles, uncooked
- 10-1/2-ounce can tomato soup
- 1/2 green pepper, chopped
- 1 cup water
- Liquid from can of peas
- 1 teaspoon EACH of sweet basil, celery seed and oregano
- 1 tablespoon Worcestershire sauce
- 2 cloves garlic, minced
- 1/2 cup catsup
- 16-ounce can lima beans, drained
- 16-ounce can peas (liquid used above)
- 16-ounce can cream style corn
- 1 cup shredded cheddar cheese

Brown beef and onions in large, deep saucepot. Add uncooked noodles, soup, green pepper, water and liquid from peas. Cover and simmer until noodles are tender, do not stir. Add spices, and remaining ingredients, except shredded cheese. Pour into large baking dish, top with cheese and bake at 350° about 35 to 40 minutes until casserole is bubbly hot and cheese is melted.

Mrs. Damon Ruggels, Columbus, Kansas

FIESTA BEEF TORTA OLE

Beef Filling:

- **2-1/2 pounds ground beef round**
- **1 package taco seasoning mix**
- **1 cup water**
- **16-ounce can refried beans**
- **4 ounces Monterey Jack cheese, grated**

Dough:

- **3-1/4 to 3-3/4 cups unbleached flour**
- **3/4 cup yellow cornmeal**
- **1/4 cup brown sugar, packed**
- **2 teaspoons garlic salt**
- **1 teaspoon taco seasoning mix**
- **2 packages active dry yeast**
- **3/4 cup milk**
- **1/3 cup water**
- **1/4 cup margarine or butter**
- **2 eggs, beaten**

Coating, Topping, Garnish:

- **2 tablespoons cornmeal**
- **2 tablespoons reserved beaten egg**
- **2 8-ounce jars taco sauce, hot or mild as preferred**
- **1 to 2 tablespoons pine nuts**
- **Shredded lettuce**
- **Cherry tomatoes**
- **Ripe olives**

Dough: In large mixer bowl, mix 3/4 cup flour, cornmeal, brown sugar, garlic salt, 1 teaspoon taco seasoning and dry yeast. In saucepan, combine milk, water and margarine or butter; heat over low heat until mixture is very warm (120° to 130°), butter does not need to be melted. Add mixture gradually to dry ingredients and beat 2 minutes at medium speed, scraping bowl occasionally. Reserve 2 tablespoons beaten egg. Add remaining eggs and 1/3 cup flour; beat at high speed 2 minutes; scraping bowl occasionally. Stir in enough additional flour to make a stiff dough. Turn onto lightly floured board; knead until smooth and elastic, 5 to 8 minutes. Place in greased bowl, cover and let rise until doubled. **Beef Filling:** Brown beef until red color disappears; drain fat, if necessary. Add remaining taco seasoning and water; simmer, stirring occasionally for 15 minutes. Stir in beans and cheese; blend well. Cool slightly. **To Assemble:** Grease 9-in. springform pan generously. Fold a 30- x 6-in. piece of heavy foil in half lengthwise. Fasten foil around top of pan to form collar extending 2-1/2-in. above rim of pan (as for a souffle); grease inside of foil also. Dust bottom and sides of pan with cornmeal; discard excess. Punch down dough; divide into 3 portions. Pat or roll each portion to a 9-in. round. Fit first round of dough into pan; press at edge to form slight rim. Spoon in half of beef filling; spreading evenly almost to edge of pan. Top with second round of dough, then remaining beef filling. Place third round of dough on top; cover and let rise in warm place until light, 25 to 35 minutes. Preheat oven to 350°. Score top of torta with sharp knife into 8 pie-shaped wedges. Brush with reserved egg; sprinkle with pine nuts. Bake 40 minutes or until deep golden brown. When almost ready to serve, heat taco sauce. **To Serve:** Remove foil and springform rim from torta; place torta on large plate. Surround with ring of shredded lettuce, garnished with cherry tomatoes and ripe olives. Place heated taco sauce in gravy boat to spoon over torta after it is cut and served. Cut in wedges as indicated. Yield 8 servings.

Mrs. Alexander DeSantis, Bethlehem, Pennsylvania
1977 National Beef Cook-Off winner.

RICE CALIENTE

1 pound ground beef
1 cup chopped onion
1 teaspoon salt
1 teaspoon garlic powder
10-ounce can green chilies and tomatoes (Ro-Tel)
2 cups cooked rice
1 cup sour cream
1 cup shredded Monterey Jack cheese
Paprika

Saute ground beef, onions and seasonings until meat loses its color and onions are glossy. Drain off fat. Chop chilies and tomatoes; add to meat mixture. Stir in rice and sour cream. Turn into greased 1-1/2-quart casserole dish; bake at 350° until mixture bubbles, about 40 minutes. Remove from oven, sprinkle with cheese and paprika. Return to oven for 5 minutes to melt cheese. Serves 6.

Mrs. Eugene Bulla, Jonesboro, Arkansas

TACO PIE

1-1/4 pounds ground beef
2 tablespoons dry taco seasoning
1/2 cup water
1/3 cup green olives, sliced
8-ounce can Pillsbury crescent rolls
2 cups crushed corn chips (Doritos)
1 cup dairy sour cream
1 cup shredded cheddar cheese

Brown beef; drain off fat. Stir in seasoning mix, water and olives; simmer 5 minutes. Press roll dough into 9-in. pie pan forming a crust. Sprinkle 1 cup crushed corn chips over bottom of crust. Spoon meat mixture into crust. Spread top with sour cream, cover with cheese then sprinkle remaining chips over top. Bake at 350° 20 to 35 minutes until brown.

Mrs. Melvin Wile, Pomeray, Iowa

IRRESISTIBLE ENCHILADAS

Pancakes:

- 6 eggs, well beaten
- 3 cups milk
- 2 cups flour
- 3/4 teaspoon salt

Meat Filling:

- 10-ounce package frozen spinach
- 1-1/2 pounds ground beef
- 1 pound pork sausage
- 1 cup chopped onions
- 1/2 cup chopped green peppers
- 2 cloves garlic, minced
- 1-1/3 tablespoons chili powder*
- 1 teaspoon salt

Sauce:

- 29 ounces meatless spaghetti sauce
- 8 ounces tomato sauce
- 1 cup water
- 1 tablespoon chili powder
- 2 cups shredded cheddar cheese

Pancakes: Combine eggs and milk, add flour and salt; beat well. Pour about 1/4 cup batter into hot, greased skillet. Spread into 6-in. pancakes. Turn pancake when top looks dry; brown lightly. Pancakes may be stacked with waxed paper between. **Yield:** About 30 pancakes. **Meat Filling:** Cook spinach, drain well and chop. Brown beef, and pork sausage. Pour off all but 1 tablespoon fat. Add onions, peppers and seasonings. *Adjust chili powder to taste. Simmer mixture 10 minutes; add spinach, mix and set aside. **Sauce:** Combine first four ingredients, again adjusting chili powder to your taste. To assemble recipe, spoon scant 1/4 cup meat mixture across center of the pancake. Fold sides over about 1/2-in. Starting at end closest to you, roll up pancake. Place in two 13- x 9-in. greased baking dishes. Divide sauce over both dishes. Top with shredded cheese. Bake at 325° for 30 minutes. **Note:** Enchiladas can be frozen. To reheat, bake at 375° 45 to 60 minutes.

Mrs. Otto Fahning, Wells, Minnesota

BREAD CRUMB COATING: *For a crispy crumb coating that's sure to stick to the meat, dip meat slices first in flour, turning to coat both sides; shake off excess flour. Then dip in beaten egg, thinned with 1 tablespoon milk or water; turn to coat both sides; allow excess egg to drip off. Then coat with seasoned bread crumbs (salt, pepper and dried herbs, such a savory, chervil, chives, basil or tarragon). Pat crumbs gently onto meat. Place on wire rack to dry or set up before frying, about 20 minutes. Do not chill meat before frying! This would tend to make it absorb an undue amount of fat when frying.*

Mrs. Glenn O. Tedrow, Fairfield, Iowa

Oriental Delicacies

HAMBURGER ORIENTAL

1 pound ground beef
2 cups celery, diagonally sliced
1 envelope onion soup mix
2 tablespoons cornstarch
1 pound can bean sprouts, drained
2 teaspoons soy sauce
2 cups water
Large can chow mein noodles OR cooked rice

Brown beef and celery until beef looses its red color. Add soup mix, cornstarch, sprouts, soy sauce and water. Bring to boil, stirring. Reduce to low heat. Cover and cook about 10 minutes, stirring occasionally. Serve over chow mein noodles or cooked rice. *Mrs. R.A. Cundall, Murray, Nebraska*

ORIENTAL BURGER JOES

1 pound ground beef
1/4 cup chopped onion
2 tablespoons butter
1 tablespoon prepared mustard
2 tablespoons tomato paste
2 tablespoons LaChoy soy sauce
1/2 teaspoon garlic powder
1/4 teaspoon pepper
1 teaspoon prepared horseradish
16-ounce can bean sprouts
1/2 cup dairy sour cream
8 hamburger buns

Saute beef and onion in butter until browned. Stir in mustard, tomato paste, soy sauce, garlic powder, pepper, horseradish and bean sprouts. Simmer, stirring occasionally for 10 minutes or until mixture is heated through. Remove from heat; stir in sour cream. Serve on buttered, toasted buns.

Charlotte Koehn, Livingston, California

ORIENTAL SPAGHETTI

1-1/2 pounds ground beef
1/2 pound bulk seasoned sausage
1 medium-sized onion, chopped
1 cup diced celery
7 ounces spaghetti, cooked
1 cup shredded cheddar cheese
1 can cream of tomato soup
1 can Chinese mixed vegetables, drained, reserve juice
4 ounces canned mushrooms, drained, reserve juice
3 tablespoons soy sauce

Brown beef, sausage and onion. Combine all ingredients except juices and soy sauce. Mix gently and place in greased baking casserole dish. Pour combined juices and soy sauce over casserole. Bake at 325° 1 hour.

Mrs. George F. Miller, Solon, Iowa

CANTONESE MEATBALLS

1 pound ground beef
1/4 cup fine dry bread crumbs
1/2 cup finely chopped onion
1 teaspoon salt
Dash pepper
2/3 cup evaporated milk
2 tablespoons butter
13-1/2-ounce can pineapple tidbits, drained, reserve juice
1-1/2 tablespoons cornstarch
2 tablespoons water
1/4 cup vinegar
1/4 cup sugar
2 teaspoons soy sauce
1 tablespoon butter
1/2 cup sliced green onions
1/2 cup green pepper strips
1 cup sliced celery
1 large tomato, cut in wedges

Combine beef, crumbs, onion, salt, pepper and milk; blend well. Shape into small meatballs. Heat 2 tablespoons butter in skillet; brown meatballs. In small bowl make a paste of cornstarch and 2 tablespoons water; add pineapple juice, vinegar, sugar and soy sauce. Pour over meatballs; bring to boil. Cover and simmer 20 minutes on low heat. Add pineapple, 1 tablespoon butter and remaining ingredients. Cover; continue cooking 10 minutes longer. Serve over hot, cooked rice. *Mrs. Alice Walker, Blue Mound, Kansas*

MOCK CHOW MEIN

2 pounds ground beef
1 cup diced celery
1 cup diced onion
10-3/4-ounce can chicken noodle soup
10-3/4-ounce can chicken rice soup
10-3/4-ounce can cream of mushroom soup
1/2 cup uncooked rice (not instant)
1 pound can peas, drained, reserve juice
3-1/2 tablespoons soy sauce
1-1/3 cups liquid (reserved pea juice plus water)
8-1/2-ounce can water chestnuts, coarsely chopped
14 ounces chow mein noodles
Salted cashews OR peanuts

Brown beef, celery and onion. Add soups, mixing to blend. Add rice, peas, soy sauce, liquid and chopped chestnuts. Pour into 4-quart casserole; bake at 350° for 1 hour, stirring once or twice during baking time. After 1 hour, sprinkle chow mein noodles and nuts over top of casserole and bake 1/2 hour more. *Ruth R. Daly, New Hope, Minnesota*

ORIENTAL HOT DISH

2 pounds ground beef
1-1/2 cups chopped onion
1 teaspoon salt
1/8 teaspoon pepper
1 can Chinese vegetables, drained, reserve juice
1-1/2 cups diced celery
8-ounce can water chestnuts, drained, sliced
8-ounce can mushrooms and juice
1 can cream of mushroom soup
1 can cream of tomato soup
1 soup can liquid (reserved vegetable juice, mushroom juice plus water)
1/4 cup soy sauce
2 cups chow mein noodles

Brown beef and onion; salt and pepper to taste. Add remaining ingredients except chow mein noodles. Mix thoroughly. Pour into large baking dish. Bake at 350° about 1 hour. Serve with chow mein noodles sprinkled over top.

Mrs. Fred Kraemer, Glencoe, Minnesota

CHINESE CASSEROLE FOR A CROWD

3 pounds ground beef
2 onions, chopped
1 green pepper, chopped
1 pound mushrooms
2 teaspoons salt
Pepper to taste
8 ounces fine egg noodles
1/2 cup chopped pimiento-stuffed olives
3 cans cream of mushroom soup
2 13-ounce cans evaporated milk, undiluted
1 can sliced water chestnuts, drained
1 cup shredded sharp cheddar cheese
1 can Chinese noodles
Slivered almonds

Brown beef. Remove from skillet to large bowl with slotted spoon. In same skillet saute onion, green pepper and sliced fresh mushrooms until tender. Add to meat, seasoning with salt and pepper to taste. Cook noodles according to directions on package, drain. Add to meat mixture. Add olives. Combine soup and milk; stirring to blend. Fold into meat mixture; add chestnuts and cheese. Place mixture into 2 13- x 9-in. baking dishes. Bake at 375° 35 minutes. Sprinkle tops of casseroles with Chinese noodles and slivered almonds. Return to oven and bake 10 minutes more to toast noodles and nuts. **Note:** This recipe freezes well.

Mrs. Mary Ellen Ade, West Lafayette, Indiana

ORIENTAL CASSEROLE

- 1 pound ground beef
- 1/3 cup chopped celery
- 1/3 cup chopped onion
- 1/4 cup chopped green pepper
- 1 cup water
- 4 tablespoons cornstarch
- 1 teaspoon sugar
- 1/4 teaspoon ground ginger
- 2 tablespoons water
- 1/4 cup soy sauce
- 16 ounces chop suey vegetables, drained
- 10 ounces frozen peas
- 1 can chow mein noodles

Brown beef, celery, onion and green pepper. Add water; bring meat mixture to slow boil. Blend cornstarch, sugar, ginger, water and soy sauce. Stir into meat mixture; cook until thickened. Add vegetables and peas. Pour into 2-quart casserole. Bake at 350° 1 hour. Top with chow mein noodles, return to oven to brown noodles, about 15 minutes.

Mrs. Alice Walker, Blue Mound, Kansas

EASY HOME-MADE NOODLES: *Add an egg to a package of pie crust mix. Roll out, cut and let dry. Noodles are quick to make and delicious!*

Mrs. C.R. Landphair, Humeston, Iowa

THAW GROUND BEEF QUICKLY: *Preheat oven to 350°, turn off heat and place package of ground beef on cookie sheet in the warmed oven. Meat will thaw quickly, ready for use.* *Mrs. Charlotte Roach, Faucett, Missouri*

SAVING MEAT LOAF: *Leftover meat loaf can become a hearty, warm meal in a hurry. After its first serving, slice into individual servings. Freeze on cookie sheet, then put in plastic bag for freezer storage. As you need it, remove as many slices as you will use.*

GLAMOROUS LEFTOVER MEAT LOAF: *Slice meat loaf, roll in buttered bread crumbs. Broil until lightly browned and serve with sauce made of 1/2 cup catsup and 1/2 cup brown sugar. (Heat the sauce until sugar dissolves, then spread over meat.)*

Italian Pizzaria

'ALIAN SPAGHETTI SAUCE

tablespoons oil
small onion, diced
pounds ground beef
cloves of garlic, minced
1-pound cans tomatoes
8-ounce can tomato sauce
small can tomato paste
cup water
3-ounce can of sliced mushrooms, drained

1/4 cup parsley flakes
1-1/2 teaspoons oregano
1 teaspoon salt
1/2 teaspoon monosodium glutamate
1/4 teaspoon thyme
1 teaspoon black pepper
1 bay leaf (optional)

ook onion and ground beef in oil. Add garlic and monosodium glutamate. a large pot mix the remaining ingredients. When onion and beef have owned, add to the sauce mixture. Cook uncovered for 2-2-1/2 hours. emove bay leaf. *Mrs. Martha Wyatt, Saltillo, Tennessee*

RESCENT ROLL LASAGNA

leat Filling:

1 pound ground beef
/4 cup chopped onion
/2 teaspoon garlic salt
1 tablespoon parsley flakes
6-ounce can tomato paste
1/2 teaspoon EACH basil, oregano, salt
Dash pepper

heese Filling:

cup cottage cheese
egg
3/4 cup shredded mozarella cheese

rust:

cans crescent rolls
slices mozarella cheese
1 tablespoon milk
1 tablespoon sesame seeds

leat Filling: Brown beef and onion; drain fat. Add remaining meat ingre-ents, simmer, uncovered 5 minutes. **Cheese Filling:** Combine ingredients. **rust:** Unroll biscuits. Place on ungreased cookie sheet overlapping edges id sealing perforations to form 15- x 13-in. rectangle. Spread half of meat ixture lengthwise down center of dough. Top meat filling with cheese fill-g. Spoon remaining meat over cheese. Place mozarella cheese slices over eat. Fold 13-in. ends of dough over filling, pinching dough to seal. Brush p with milk and sprinkle with sesame seed. Bake at 375° 20 to 25 minutes ntil crust is golden brown. *Alta Mullet, Sugarcreek, Ohio*

MANICOTTI

1 pound ground beef
1 onion, chopped
1 clove garlic, minced
8 ounces shredded mozzarella cheese*
1/2 cup bread crumbs
1/4 cup chopped parsley
1 egg
Salt and pepper
1 box (12 shells) manicotti macaroni
2 15-ounce jars prepared spaghetti sauce
1/2 cup grated Parmesan chees

Brown beef, onion and garlic; cool. Stir in cheese. (*1 cup ricotta and 1 cu mozarella may be used). Stir in crumbs, parsley and egg. Season to taste Cook manicotti shells according to directions on package—do not overcook Stuff shells with meat mixture, handling carefully. Spoon half of spaghet sauce over bottom of 13- x 9-in. baking dish. Arrange stuffed manicotti shell over sauce. Pour remaining sauce over shells. Sprinkle with Parmesa cheese. Bake at 350° to 400° oven 20 to 30 minutes.

Mrs. Ruth Rohloff, Francesville, Indian

LASAGNA PIZZA

1 package Pillsbury hot roll mix
1 package dry Italian seasoning
1 pound ground beef
1 onion, chopped
15 ounces tomato sauce
6 ounces cottage cheese
8 ounces mozarella cheese, shredded

Add 1 tablespoon dry Italian seasoning mix to roll mix, then mix according t directions on box. Spread in greased pizza pan (do not allow dough to rise Bake at 350° 10 minutes. Meanwhile brown beef and onion; drain fat. Ad remaining Italian seasoning mix and tomato sauce. Simmer 10 minute Spread cottage cheese on baked crust, top with ground beef; bake at 350 15-20 minutes. Sprinkle mozarella cheese over top, bake 5 minutes more.

Mrs. Randy Koehl, Hancock, Minneso

CRUSTY PIZZA HOT DISH

2 packages refrigerator crescent rolls
1-1/2 pounds ground beef
1 onion, diced
8 ounces pizza sauce
1 teaspoon oregano or to taste
8 ounces shredded cheddar cheese
8 ounces shredded mozzarella cheese

nroll 1 package dough leaving seams intact; press into 13- x 9-in. pan. 'own ground beef and onion until meat loses its pink color; spread over ough. Combine sauce, oregano and cheeses; spread over meat. Cover with ust of remaining roll dough. Bake, uncovered at 350° 30 to 35 minutes.

Mrs. Dwaine D. Kauffman, Minot, North Dakota

IANT PIZZA SANDWICH

'2 pound ground beef
'4 cup chopped onion
'4 cup chopped green pepper
nall can sliced mushrooms, drained
2 tablespoons sliced pimiento or stuffed green olives
1/2 teaspoon oregano
4 ounces shredded mozzarella cheese, divided
2 10-in. frozen cheese pizzas

iute meat, onions, green pepper, mushrooms, olives and oregano until eat is browned. Stir in 1/2 cup of cheese. Place one pizza on baking sheet. oon hot meat mixture evenly over pizza, top with second pizza, crust side). Cover with foil, bake at 375° 15 minutes. Remove foil, continue baking 10 inutes more. Sprinkle with remaining cheese; bake 5 minutes more. Serves <.

Mrs. Gretta Christen, Roggen, Colorado

UICK LASAGNE

1 pound ground beef
1/2 clove garlic
1/2 teaspoons dried basil
3/4 teaspoon salt
16 ounces spaghetti sauce
3 cups wide noodles
1/2 cups creamed cottage cheese
1/4 cup grated Parmesan cheese
1 tablespoon dried parsley flakes
1 egg
1/2 teaspoon salt
1/4 teaspoon pepper
8 ounces mozzarella cheese, shredded

large skillet or electric fry pan, brown beef and garlic. Add seasonings and aghetti sauce. Cover and simmer 10 minutes. Meanwhile cook noodles in ghtly salted boiling water until tender; drain. Combine cottage cheese with armesan, parsley, egg, salt and pepper. Add cooked noodles and cheese ixture to meat; stir lightly to blend. Cover and simmer about 15 minutes. op with mozzarella cheese, cover and heat until cheese is melted.

Mrs. David Heinrich, Adrian, North Dakota

PIZZA LOAF

1-1/2 pounds ground beef
3/4 cup quick cooking oats
1 egg
1-1/2 teaspoons salt
3/4 teaspoon oregano
8 ounces tomato sauce
1/4 cup chopped onion
1 tablespoon Worcestershire sauce
1-1/2 teaspoons Accent seasoning, optional
1/4 teaspoon pepper
6 ounces sliced mozzarella cheese

Combine all ingredients except cheese. Divide meat mixture into thirds. P 1/3 mixture in bottom of 9-1/2- x 5- x 3-in. loaf pan; cover with half cheese. Repeat layers ending with meat. Bake at 350° 1 hour. Serves 5 to

Mrs. Leonard T. Pohlkamp, Jr., Pierz, Minneso

PIZZA BURGERS

12-ounce can luncheon meat
2 pounds mozzarella cheese
3 pounds hamburger
15-ounce can pizza sauce
Oregano and sage to taste
25 hamburger buns
Parmesan cheese

Grind luncheon meat and cheese through meat grinder. Mix with hamburg and pizza sauce. Adjust seasoning with more oregano and sage, if desire Spread on halves of hamburger buns; broil about 15 minutes. Sprinkle top burger with Parmesan cheese when filling is almost done. **Note:** Mixtu may be frozen in suitable amounts for future use.

Mrs. Elmer Klug, Mequon, Wiscons

PIZZA CASSEROLE

8 ounces spaghetti, cooked
2 pounds ground beef
1 chopped onion
1 can tomato soup
1 can cream of mushroom soup
2 teaspoons Worcestershire sauce
1 teaspoon chili powder
1/4 teaspoon pepper
1 teaspoon oregano
1/2 teaspoon salt
4 ounces sliced mozzarella cheese

Brown ground beef and onion. Combine with remaining ingredients, exce cheese. Place in large casserole dish and bake at 350° 45 minutes. Spre cheese over casserole and bake 10 minutes more.

Mrs. Kenneth D. Schrock, Congerville, Illinc

LASAGNA

- 1 pound ground beef
- 1/4 cup chopped onion
- 1 clove garlic, minced
- 6 ounces tomato paste
- 3-1/2 cups tomato juice or sauce
- 1/2 teaspoon pepper
- 2 teaspoons salt
- 1/4 teaspoon basil
- 1/2 teaspoon oregano
- 8 ounces lasagna noodles
- 8 ounces sliced mozzarella cheese
- 3/4 pound riccotta OR cottage cheese
- 1/2 cup Parmesan cheese

Cook lasagna noodles in boiling salted water until tender. (Add 1 tablespoon oil to water to prevent noodles from sticking together.) Drain; spread out on waxed paper. Brown beef, onion and garlic. Add tomato paste, juice and seasonings. Simmer, covered about 15 minutes. In 13- x 9- x 2-in. baking dish, assemble layers of 1/2 meat mixture, noodles, cottage cheese, mozzarella. Repeat with remaining half of ingredients, reserving enough meat sauce for thin layer over top. Dust with Parmesan cheese. Bake at 350° about 30 minutes or until dish is hot and bubbly.

Mrs. Karen E. Kauffman, Dornsife, Pennsylvania

RAVIOLI CASSEROLE

- 1 pound ground beef
- 1/2 cup chopped onion
- 1 clove garlic, minced
- 10-ounce package frozen chopped spinach
- 16 ounces spaghetti sauce with mushrooms
- 8 ounces tomato sauce
- 6 ounces tomato paste
- 1/2 teaspoon salt
- 1/8 teaspoon pepper
- 7 ounces macaroni, cooked
- 1 cup sharp cheddar cheese
- 1/2 cup soft bread crumbs
- 2 eggs, well beaten
- 1/4 cup salad oil

Brown beef, onion and garlic; drain fat. Cook spinach; drain, reserving liquid. Add water to spinach liquid to equal 1 cup. Add liquid, spaghetti sauce, tomato sauce and paste, salt and pepper to meat mixture. Simmer 10 minutes. In mixing bowl, combine cooked spinach, cooked macaroni, cheese, crumbs, eggs and salad oil; mix well. Spread into greased 13- x 9- x -in. baking dish. Top with meat sauce. Bake at 350° about 30 minutes or until casserole is hot and bubbly. Let stand 10 minutes before serving. Serves 8.

Mrs. Martha Bitter, Madera, California

DIET LASAGNE

1 pound ground beef
1/8 cup onion flakes
8 ounces tomato sauce
1 teaspoon basil
1 teaspoon parsley flakes
1/4 teaspoon oregano
Dash garlic salt
Dash pepper
4 ounces mushrooms, drained
10 ounces frozen chopped spinach, thawed
8 ounces low fat cottage chees
4 ounces mozzarella cheese

Brown meat and onion flakes; drain fat. Add tomato sauce, basil, parsley oregano, salt and pepper. Add mushrooms. Squeeze liquid from spinach combine with cottage cheese. Cut mozzarella cheese in strips. In 11- x 7-in baking dish layer meat mixture, spinach-cheese mixture and mozzarell cheese. Repeat layers. Bake at 375° 20 minutes. Let stand about 5 to 1 minutes before serving. *Mrs. Elvis Brassfield, Jefferson, Wisconsi*

ZUBEEFI

2-1/2 pounds ground beef
2 medium zucchini
Salt and pepper
1/2 cup olive oil
3 medium onions, sliced
1 green pepper, chopped
1/3 clove garlic, chopped
3 tablespoons butter
2 teaspoons salt
1/2 teaspoon pepper
1 tablespoon oregano
6 ounces tomato paste
1 cup small curd cottage cheese
2 cups grated mozzarella cheese
1/4 cup grated Parmesan chees
4 stuffed green olives, sliced
Butter

Slice one zucchini thinly, season with salt and pepper; fry in olive oil. Plac zucchini in a buttered 3-quart casserole. Fry onions, green pepper and garli in butter; remove and add to zucchini. Brown beef in frying pan, pour o drippings. Stir salt, pepper, oregano and tomato paste into meat; cook slow ly 3 minutes. Add meat mixture to zucchini; cool 5 minutes. Add cottag cheese, mix well. Sprinkle mozzarella cheese on top; cover and bake at 350 for 30 minutes. Remove cover; sprinkle with Parmesan cheese; place slice olives on top. Bake uncovered 15 minutes. Slice remaining zucchini, saute i butter and place on top of casserole. Yield: 6 to 8 servings.

Dr. Sam Tornik, Plain City, Ohi
Second place winner 1977 National Beef Cook-O

IZZA HOT DISH

1 pound ground beef
/4 cup chopped green pepper
/4 cup chopped onion
20 ounces pizza sauce
/2 teaspoon onion salt
/4 teaspoon pepper
7 ounces spiral macaroni, cooked
7-ounce can mushrooms
2 ounces sliced olives
1 small can shrimp, optional
1/4 pound shredded cheddar cheese
1/4 pound shredded mozzarella cheese
1/4 cup grated Parmesan cheese

aute beef, green pepper and onion until meat is browned. Add pizza sauce nd spices; simmer about 15 minutes. Cook and drain noodles. Spread oodles in bottom of greased 13- x 9- x 2-in. baking dish. Pour meat sauce ver noodles. Spread mushrooms, olives and shrimp over sauce. Sprinkle heeses over top. Cover and bake at 350° 35 minutes. Uncover and bake 10 inutes more. *Mrs. Peggy Legler, Evansville, Wisconsin*

OUR PIZZA

ornmeal

atter:
cup flour
teaspoon salt
teaspoon oregano OR Italian seasoning
1/8 teaspoon pepper
2 eggs
2/3 cup milk

opping:
1 pound ground beef
/4 cup chopped onion
1 cup mushrooms, sliced
1 cup pizza sauce
1 cup shredded mozzarella cheese

rease and dust jelly roll pan with cornmeal. **Batter:** Combine ingredients; eat until smooth. Pour into pan, spreading in thin layer to cover bottom. **opping:** Brown meat and onion. Sprinkle over batter. Add remaining ingreients in layers over meat. Bake at 425° 20 to 30 minutes.

Mrs. LeeAnn Smucker, Harrisburg, Oregon

OUNTER TOP PIZZA: *When cooking only one pizza, save some energy y cooking it in your electric fry pan. The results will be a perfectly done ust and soft, gooey cheese. Dorothy S. Hansen, Washington, Wisconsin*

Ground Beef Stock Pot

BEEF DOGS KABOBS

1 pound ground beef
/4 cup milk
1 small onion, chopped
/2 cup bread OR cracker crumbs
Salt and pepper
1 egg
6 frankfurters
6 slices bacon

Barbecue Sauce:
/4 cup catsup
/4 cup molasses
2 tablespoons vinegar
1/4 cup sugar

Mix beef, milk, onion, crumbs, seasoning and egg. Divide meat mixture into portions. Wrap each portion around a frankfurter, covering completely. Wrap slice of bacon around beef-dog, securing ends with wooden toothpicks. Broil on grill or in the oven until done, basting with barbecue sauce several times. **Barbecue Sauce:** Combine ingredients, simmer about 5 minutes.

Mrs. Pat A. Miller, Oregon, Wisconsin

RANCH BEEF BREAD

1 cup water
1/2 cup sugar
1 cup cooked, ground roast beef
1 cup raisins
2 packages dry yeast
1/2 cup warm water
1-1/2 cups potato water
3 tablespoons shortening
1 cup all-bran cereal
1 tablespoon molasses
2 cups whole wheat flour
2 cups white flour
3 teaspoons salt
4 cups white flour
1/2 cup chopped walnuts

Boil water, sugar, cooked ground beef and raisins; cool. Soak yeast in warm water. Add to cooled beef mixture. Add potato water, shortening, all-bran, molasses, 2 cups *each* wheat and white flour. Mix with spoon and let rise 10 minutes. Add salt, 4 cups white flour and nuts. Knead until satiny. Let rise in warm place until doubled. Punch down; let rise again 20 minutes. Shape into 3 loaves and let rise until dough nearly reaches top of pans. Bake at 350° 40 minutes.

Frieda Bowman, Alliance, Nebraska

MINCEMEAT

1/2 pound ground beef
1 cup water
3/4 cup pickle juice
1 teaspoon salt
3 cups raw apple
1 cup raisins
1/2 lemon and peel
1/2 orange and peel
1-1/4 cups sugar
1 tablespoon cinnamon
1/4 teaspoon cloves

Boil water and beef for 30 minutes. Meanwhile grind or chop fine the apple (raisins may be left whole) lemon and orange with peels. Add fruits and remaining ingredients to beef. Cook until thickened about 45 minutes.

Mrs. Donna DeBower, Allison, Iowa

MINCEMEAT CRUMB CAKE

3 cups flour
1 teaspoon baking soda
1 teaspoon baking powder
1 cup sugar
1 cup butter
1 cup dairy sour cream
1 cup milk
1 teaspoon vanilla
2 eggs
2-1/2 cups mincemeat (recipe above)

Crumb Topping:
6 tablespoons flour
2 tablespoons sugar
2 tablespoons brown sugar
1/2 teaspoon cinnamon
3 tablespoons butter

Combine flour, baking soda and powder, and sugar; cut in butter. Add sour cream, milk, vanilla and eggs; beat well. Spread half of batter in 13- x 9-inch greased and floured pan. Spoon mincemeat evenly over batter. Cover with remaining batter. **Crumb Topping:** Mix dry ingredients; cut in butter. Sprinkle evenly over cake. Bake at 350° 40 to 45 minutes. **Note:** Allow cake to mellow 1 day before serving. May be topped with whipped cream or ice cream if desired.

Mrs. Donna DeBower, Allison, Iowa

GROUND BEEF POULTRY STUFFING

Giblets from fowl
1/2 pound ground beef
1 medium-sized onion, minced
1/2 cup butter
2 large potatoes, grated
1-1/2 pounds day old bread, cubed
2 eggs, slightly beaten
1 cup chopped celery
1 teaspoon poultry seasoning

Boil giblets in lightly salted boiling water until tender. Remove from broth; hop fine. Reserve broth. Brown beef and onion in butter; add potatoes and simmer lightly. Pour reserved broth over bread cubes, add eggs, mix lightly. Combine bread mixture, beef mixture, celery and seasoning. Correct seasonng with salt and pepper to taste. If mixture is not moist enough, add small amount of beef broth, cream or water. Stuff fowl.

Mrs. Delores Baumgardt, Hector, Minnesota

BEEF AND POTATO ROLL

-1/2 pounds ground beef
1/4 cup dry bread crumbs
1 egg
1/2 teaspoon salt
2 cups mashed potatoes
2 hard cooked eggs, chopped
1/3 cup salad dressing
1/3 cup grated Parmesan cheese
1/4 cup finely chopped celery
2 tablespoons minced onion
Dash pepper

Sauce:
1 cup salad dressing
1/3 cup milk
2 tablespoons minced onion

Mix beef, crumbs, egg and salt. Set aside. Combine mashed potatoes, hard cooked eggs, salad dressing, cheese, celery, onions and pepper. Spread or pat meat in 14- x 8-in. rectangle on large piece of waxed paper or foil. Spread potato mixture over meat. Roll up jelly roll fashion using paper to help roll ightly. Cover; chill 2 hours or overnight. Slice roll into 6 portions. Bake on broiler rack at 350° 25 to 30 minutes. **Sauce:** Combine ingredients; cook, stirring, just to warm. Spoon over meat slices when served.

Angie Stewart, Bloomington, Nebraska

BEEF DROP COOKIES

1 cup ground beef
2 cups brown sugar, packed
1 cup shortening
2 eggs, slightly beaten
1/2 cup buttermilk OR sour milk
1 teaspoon salt
1/2 teaspoon baking soda
1 teaspoon baking powder
3 cups flour

Brown beef until it loses its color. Or grind leftover, cooked roast beef. Cream sugar and shortening, add eggs; beat until fluffy. Add beef and buttermilk. Sift dry ingredients, add to beef mixture. Drop by teaspoonfuls onto greased baking sheet. Bake at 350° 10 to 12 minutes.

Mrs. Michael L. Ditmore, Pampa, Texas

MEAT ROLL

2 eggs, beaten
1 cup soft bread crumbs
3/4 cup tomato juice
2 tablespoons snipped parsley
1/2 teaspoon oregano
1/4 teaspoon salt
1/4 teaspoon pepper
1/4 teaspoon garlic salt
2 pounds ground beef
8 slices boiled ham
1-1/2 cups shredded mozzarella cheese
3 slices mozzarella cheese

Combine eggs, bread crumbs, tomato juice, parsley, oregano, salt, peppe and garlic salt. Stir into beef, mix well. Pat meat into 12- x 10-in. rectangle Arrange ham on top of meat, leaving small margin around edges. Sprinkl shredded cheese over ham. Roll up jelly roll fashion, seal edges and ends Place meat roll, seam side down, on baking pan. Bake at 350° for 1 hour Place cheese wedges over top of roll, return to oven 5 minutes until chees melts.

Josie Pritchard, Atkinson, Illinoi

BEEFED-UP BROWNIES

1/2 cup ground beef
3 eggs
1 cup sugar
1/2 teaspoon salt
1 teaspoon vanilla
1/2 cup butter
2 squares unsweetened chocolate
3/4 cup flour
1/2 teaspoon baking powder
1/2 cup nutmeats

Frosting:
1 square unsweetened chocolate
1/4 cup butter
2 cups confectioner's sugar
Milk

Cook ground beef until it loses its color; drain. Or grind leftover cooked roas beef. Beat eggs, sugar, salt and vanilla until fluffy. Add beef. Melt butter an chocolate, cool. Stir into egg mixture. Add remaining ingredients; beat unt smooth. Pour into greased 12- x 8-in. baking dish. Bake at 350° 20 minutes **Frosting:** Melt chocolate and butter, cool slightly. Add confectioner's suga and 1 tablespoon of milk at a time, beating until frosting is spreadable.

Mrs. Carole Benke, Waucoma, Iow

Index